The Reflex

Activate Thoughts, Words and Actions to Achieve Your Goals

CHRIS WEILER

MythBuster Media Inc.
Chicago

Copyright © 2015 by Chris Weiler

Books may be purchased in quantity and/or special sales by contacting the publisher.

Mythbuster Media Inc.
Chicago
sales@MythBusterMedia.com
www.MythBusterMedia.com

Library of Congress Control Number: 2014920628

ISBN 0989179621
ISBN 978-0-9891796-2-1

Cover Design: Gion-Per Marxer - Gion-Per@beecoding.com

Contents

Acknowledgements

Gen Khedrub

Wangdon

Geshe Kelsang Gyatso

Thank you for helping me navigate the Buddhist waters.

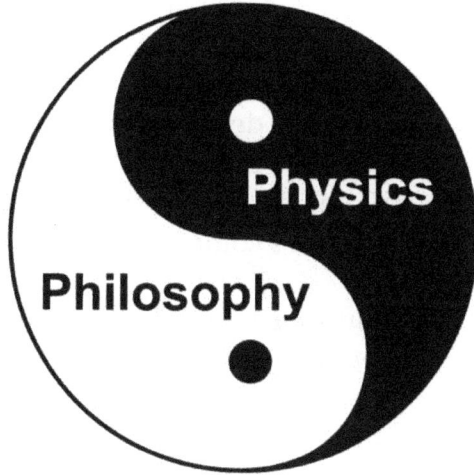

My background is in philosophy and physics. Simply put, philosophy is the science of how to think about things and physics is the science of how things work. Continuing my education through the National Academy of Sports Medicine provided a lens for me to focus and apply my background in how to develop the body and mind to improve performance.

Enhancing performance in any area of life, involves constructing habits and behaviors that support our goals, while deconstructing habits and behaviors that oppose our efforts. For many of us, achieving meaningful goals is what produces a happy, inspired and fulfilled life.

In addition to good genetics, a common characteristic of all strong competitive athletes, is the daily practice of self-managing their bodies, minds and hearts. These tools of self-management support the athlete's physical, mental and emotional state, which provides the necessary platform to continue maximizing development and progress. Every serious coach, trainer and athlete, understands how vital these practices are in keeping the athlete on track, and supporting the athlete's competitive goals.

It did not occur to me until a conversation I had with one of my non-athlete clients that the performance model I use with athletes is a model that anyone and everyone can use to help achieve whatever is meaningful in their own lives.

My client, we'll call her Jane, works for M&M Mars/Wrigley company. Her company chose to dismantle and entirely rebuild their worldwide compensation and benefits structure, processes and programs - a huge project. One day Jane was describing to me the stress and pressure the international team that was assigned to this project was under. At this point the team had been at it for over six months, with no end in sight. It was like trying to assemble a jigsaw puzzle with pieces that continually changed their shape during construction and no longer fit together, which created seemingly perpetual cycles of deconstruction and reconstruction.

This type of start, stop, tear down, re-build dynamic breaks momentum, which as you can imagine, begins to wear you down as it increases frustration and discontent. Jane was interested in looking for solutions that could help this team *weather the storm and stay the course.*

I described to Jane the physical, mental and emotional processes this team was enduring and began to think out loud about ways to help them. Jane responded by saying, *they need to hear this,* and asked me to present this to the team. An opportunity to present to a Fortune 100 company, hmm... what to do? Of course I said yes! However, my next words to Jane were, *Are you sure? You know me, I'm not politically correct - I like to shoot straight.* To my surprise, Jane immediately responded by saying, *oh no, they are tired of the suits coming in with their standard, predictable format. You will be very refreshing.*

So, I was hired by M&M Mars/Wrigley company to present on performance, stress and productivity. This of course meant I needed to create a process to present. Proving once again, that necessity is truly the mother of invention. From my perspective, presentations or seminars are not especially useful in modifying habits and behaviors, unless the participants can walk away with an actionable plan they are able to understand and implement.

Therefore, to meet the challenge of addressing these issues at their root level, I developed a performance model called **The Reflex.** The simple, daily, actionable steps of **The Reflex,** modifies our reflexively conditioned responses to people, places and circumstances. This conditioned, reflexive response cycle, can be interrupted and overwritten with new reflexes, which support habits to improve performance and succeed in our goals.

For the past 20 years I have specialized in athletic performance, development and rehabilitation. More recently, I have expanded my concept of performance to include how we perform in all areas of life, to achieve personally meaningful goals. Your ability to achieve any goal, is the direct result of your conditioned behaviors and habits. Identifying and understanding your true nature or Authentic Self, enables the creation of behaviors and habits to support goals that are aligned with your Authentic Self, making them personally meaningful to you. Many find this process leads to happy and fulfilled lives.

My *Aha* moment came when I realized everywhere we go and in everything we do, each one of us carries the 3 most important elements that contribute to our success in any area of life - the Mind, Body and Heart. Whether succeeding in athletics, education, relationships, personal or work life, it is the Mind, Body and Heart that determine the quality of our results, as they are what create and condition our behaviors and habits.

I was incredibly excited by this concept of the Mind, Body and Heart, because at this level we are all equal. Without exception, every sentient being on this planet has a Mind, Body and Heart. It is not relevant that the capacity of each individual Mind, Body and Heart are not equal, but merely that we all have access to the same tools and foundational building blocks as everyone else. No one is missing these tools from their life's toolbox. This is crucial to understand, because success and happiness in all aspects of life, personal, spiritual, physical and professional, are the result of how we access and apply the Mind, Body and Heart.

The Reflex was created through a fusion of my experiences in, and the core principles of, athletic development, behavioral science, Buddhism, philosophy, and physics. I distilled these core principles into a few quick and easy steps, that produce swift and profound results. Simply follow the steps in **The Reflex** to improve performance and success in most any area of life.

I don't believe that shortcuts, often indicated by terms such as *Tips, Tricks or Hacks,* are useful for any meaningful, lasting behavioral changes. Habits and behaviors that contribute to our happiness and success, require a process driven strategy to create change at their reflexive, root level. I designed **The Reflex** to work at this root level.

It is crucial to understand we can't directly achieve goals or create happiness, but must create the causes or conditions for it. Happiness is not something you go out and get, acquire or *just be* by putting a smile on your face or thinking happy thoughts. Rather, happiness is the indirect by-product, condition or end result of our Thoughts, Words and Actions, which either support or oppose our happiness. **The Reflex** shows you how to reflexively generate Thoughts and Words to take action on your goals.

My objective, to provide a simple model anyone can use to improve performance and success in life. Think of **The Reflex** as your missing link to developing meaningful, lasting habits and behaviors, to support a successful, happy life.

Introduction

In our technology driven world, we are conditioned to give our power for achieving our goals, to things outside of our bodies, hearts and minds. If you want to de-stress, lose weight, get fit, be happy, make a habit, break a habit, or find love - I'm sure there's an *App for that*!

The problem is that lasting changes to behaviors and habits are developed inside the person, not outside. Sure, the catalyst for change can be external, but for it to stick and change behavior, your *reflex*, it must be internalized along with choices and actions that support the care and feeding of the new habit.

This book is about how to create habits and behaviors that support achieving personally meaningful goals, to pave the pathway to rich, fulfilled, happy lives. The challenge is that many of us are conditioned from a young age to live the scripted life of a consumer, marking off on our *happiness* and *fulfilled-life* checklist... education, career, house, spouse, kids, cars, pets and so forth. Yet, in acquiring these things, many still find themselves living unfulfilled, unhappy lives.

So we drink the new Kool-Aid, and jump on the technology bandwagon, in an attempt to extract happiness and boost our *Social Currency* through the latest mobile device. Although technology provides benefits, it more often serves to distract us from truly examining ourselves, and discovering what we need to support personal happiness.

For those who unplug, raise their heads and look around, the age old, burning questions still persist.

What do I do I now?   Is this all there is?   Is this all I am?

This book will help you identify who you are as an individual, your Authentic Self, which is often quite different than society's conditioned, Consumer Self. **The Reflex** will then help you create Thoughts, Words and Actions that align with your Authentic Self, to achieve personally meaningful, relevant goals. It is through this process **The Reflex** will help guide you to personal fulfillment and happiness.

The Reflex can help you lose weight, ease stress, inhibit procrastination, increase motivation, empower relationships, enhance decision making processes to thrive at work and home, and discover a meaningful, happy life. Whether creating habits to power success, or breaking habits such as smoking, fear, anger, or feelings of depression (yes, these are habits too), **The Reflex** will guide you to your destination.

The Reflex is designed to address any habit, large or small, that decreases the happiness or quality of your life, or the lives of others around you. This includes seemingly insignificant habits, such as leaving the toilet seat up, toothpaste cap off, or leaving a messy ketchup cap for someone else to deal with. *The devil is in the details and so is happiness.*

This book will guide you through 4 actionable steps enabling you to break habits that oppose your goals, while creating habits that support achieving your ends. Two of these steps are tiny actions that can be performed anywhere, and no one else can see, yet generate profound results.

You can expect **The Reflex** to help you create powerful course corrections in your daily life, which enable you to successfully navigate your way to an energized, meaningful, balanced, and fulfilled life.

Behind the scenes, at the root level, successful behavioral change through **The Reflex**, looks like this:

1. **Discovery.** Action that exposes the deposits in your mind that oppose the preferred behavior.

2. **Subconscious "House Cleaning."** Process driven exercise to loosen those deposits and "clear your mind."

3. **Cognitive Replacement and Restructuring.** Specific actions that create deposits to support the new behavior.

a. The conscious mind references the subconscious mind for most of our Thoughts, Words and Actions. Why? Reflexive responses take a few hundred milliseconds. Conscious thought is much slower.

b. Our past and current Thoughts, Words and Actions are deposited in the subconscious mind, where they are reflexively used to shape our future Thoughts, Words and Actions.

c. These deposits need to be aligned with our Guiding Principles, to support our Thoughts, Words and Actions or they will oppose our goals, performance and happiness.

d. Much like a checking account, whatever deposits have been made to the subconscious, are what is available for the conscious mind to withdraw - good or bad.

e. To change the behavior, you must change the habit. To change the habit you must go through a process that enables you to make deposits to your subconscious, which support the behavioral change you want to see. This is what **The Reflex** does.

NOTE: 1

My liberal use of capitalization, bold text and italics are meant to help reinforce important terms and concepts. My objective is to help them stick and become reflexively available in your mind - especially your subconscious mind.

NOTE: 2

The first chapter of this book is written as a quick start, *how to* guide. Chapters 3-7 cover each step of The Reflex in detail. This includes more in-depth guidance, personal experiences and real world applications of **The Reflex**, written in a conversational style. Chapters 8 and 9 have a different feel and tone as they reveal the two most significant reasons many of us struggle with habits and behaviors that oppose our goals, success and happiness.

Let's Get Started!

Chapter 1

The Reflex

Efficiency is an important principle in my life. The time I spend doing anything is deducted from the balance of time I have left to live. Rather than a dark perspective, it helps keep me connected to Thoughts, Words and Actions that add passion and joy to my life.

My *Efficiency Principle* is also reflected in the way I structured this book, which will greatly benefit many of you. I am going to give you **The Reflex** upfront, in the first chapter, without having to read the entire book. Afterwards, you will have 2 options, either of which is fine.

1. Stop reading, close the book, and immediately begin applying **The Reflex**.

2. Continue reading to understand exactly how **The Reflex** works, and the thinking that supports it.

The choice is yours.

THE REFLEX

1. Check Your Mind

2. Acts of Compassion

3. Compose Yourself

Simply following the 3 steps above, three or more times per week, will guide you through a process that creates lasting changes in habits that support your happiness. Addressing the root that supports your reflexive behavior is the most powerful action you can take to improve performance in any area of your life.

How we perform in relationships, work, sticking to resolutions, and achieving our goals are mostly the result of, and reinforced by, a conditioned, reflexive response cycle in our subconscious. **The Reflex** not only breaks this cycle, but enables you to write and program new reflexes that have the power to support the change you desire.

The first thing, is to make the first thing, the first thing.*

The home you live in is built on and supported by a foundation. This foundation provides a stable base that anchors your home to the earth. If the small effort was taken to lay a proper and solid foundation, you can feel more confident that it will support the long term enjoyment of your home.

Not limited to home construction, the concept of foundational support is reflected in some of the most important areas of our lives, including relationships, education and career. Having a stable foundation that anchors us to our goals, helps support the creation of habits and behaviors to achieve happy, fulfilled and inspired lives.

The 3 steps of **The Reflex** rests on the foundation of your **Guiding Principle(s)**. So, before we begin with Step 1 of The Reflex, it is important for you to establish and name a personal **Guiding Principle**. Simply state a concept, principle, ideal or way of being that will enable you to achieve your goals and/or lifestyle. **Guiding Principles** are best expressed as value driven statements such as, Family First, Education First, Career First, How Can I Serve You, or Pay it Forward. Your **Guiding Principle** will represent a priority in your life, enabling the empowerment of both yourself and others.

---

*The late great Stephen Covey

One of my **Guiding Principles** is what I call, **The** *thing* **Has No Power - You Do!** I don't give my power for doing, creating, communicating, exercising , educating or living my life in general to things - tools, devices, processes, systems, programs or technology. The *thing*, the tool, cannot give you anything on its own until it is acted upon by the user. What exists in the Mind, Body and Heart, guides us in the application of how the *thing* is used, and therefore, determines the quality of what is expressed or built. This is also true for **The Reflex**. Unable to act on its own, **The Reflex** requires active participation by you to power it.

The *thing* **Has No Power - You Do,** is a fixed point of reference to help guide the creation of Thoughts, Words and Actions that support my objectives and lifestyle. My **Guiding Principle** provides a powerful perspective that helps shape the way I see the world, by filtering out the irrelevant noise of our consumer driven society, which can distract me from my goals and dilute my happiness. My **Guiding Principle** helps empower myself and others on a daily basis.

Choose Your Guiding Principle

What is your fixed point of reference that will help attract Thoughts, Words and Actions to stay the course in achieving your lifestyle goals? Don't worry about choosing a perfect one, as you can always modify it later. We will also cover this in more depth in Chapter 2. For now simply go with your reflex. What is your first thought or feeling that is triggered when asked to choose a **Guiding Principle**?

Step 1

How it Works

This is performed silently, so it can be done anywhere, anytime. Simply **Check Your Mind** to discover what you think and feel at any given moment, but especially when you feel stressed or conflicted between your goals, and a habit or response that does not support your goal. Simply ask yourself, *will my next Thoughts, Words and Actions support or oppose my Guiding Principle and goal*? Whether it supports or opposes, how do you feel about your answer.

Perhaps you are trying to diet and know you should be following a proper nutrition model, like the one found in my nutrition book **The 3/4 Rule**. However, you are craving foods that don't support or may sabotage your diet goals. This is the time to **Check Your Mind** and discover the thoughts and feelings that drive and nourish those cravings. Whatever thoughts and feelings you discover - name them.

The next step is to decide if you like what you think or feel. There is no right or wrong answer, simply what is right or wrong for YOU. Perhaps you have been eating a balanced diet and meeting your exercise goals for the past 3 weeks. So, you **Check Your Mind** and discover you feel pretty good about your craving for that 600 calorie dessert. Since how you feel is in alignment with your proposed action, you need not fear your indulgence undermining your goal. However, if you don't feel good yet still submit to your craving, you are reinforcing habits that may sabotage your efforts and set you up for failure, as you are not being true to your Authentic Self.

Perhaps you feel guilt or resentment at the thought of giving in to your craving. Guilt because you feel as if you are cheating, while resentful of your situation. Simply shift your attention away from YOU as you apply step two - commit an **Act of Compassion.** Name a thought or feeling that opposes your feelings of guilt or resentment and supports the reflexive behaviors you want to reinforce. Opposing resentment includes being helpful and kind. Now, take some action that expresses that opposing thought or feeling.

You can't simply rely on an intellectual, or objective justification, as the power lies in how you *feel*, and you need to *feel good* about it. How we feel about our Thoughts, Words and Actions is how we align and unite the Mind, Body and Heart, as we condition them to best support us in the future.

Why it Works

We need to synchronize our habits and actions with what is written in our subconscious minds. If there is not a script that reflexively cues you to take action in support of your goals, failure becomes more likely. **Checking Your Mind** breaks your reflexive response pattern. This action increases the gap between moments, and the interval between one reflexive response and the next. Questioning how you think and feel requires you to be present and in the moment, enabling you to uncover and address the root of any self-sabotaging behavior.

From productivity at work, to communication issues with family, friends, co-workers, bosses or employees, to challenges with anger, stress or depression, to problems with personal finance, **Checking Your Mind** will unveil the subconscious triggers that derail optimum performance, to help you navigate more efficiently throughout your day.

Increasing efficiency enables you to expend less effort and energy to achieve greater levels of productivity, with the least amount of physical, mental and emotional wear and tear.

Step 2
(Acts of Compassion)

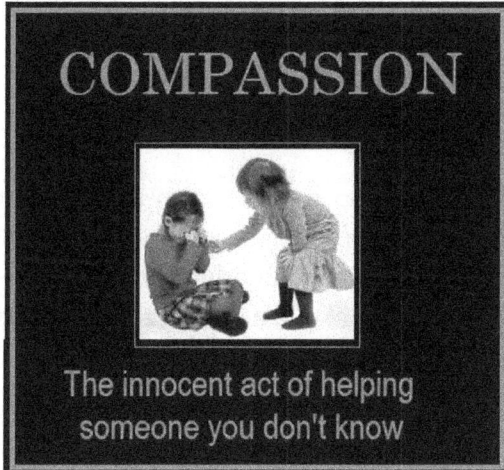

COMPASSION

The innocent act of helping
someone you don't know

How it Works

Lift up your head, open your eyes and heart, and look around you. What is one small act you can perform that is for the benefit of another living organism? That's right, humans, animals, plants, trees, and insects are all examples of living, sentient organisms you can perform **Acts of Compassion** on.

A kind act or thought is all this requires, such as helping someone with a physical task, or silently wishing the day improves for the driver receiving a speeding ticket. Simply make eye contact, smile and say hello to a stranger as you pass by. So easy, yet at times, so hard.

Why it Works

Acts of Compassion are powerful, yet simple actions that require you to look outside of your own needs, wants and concerns, by putting your *attention* on the *intention* of giving to another person. **Acts of Compassion** are what fuel the engine of **The Reflex.**

Think of this process as a mini intervention, disrupting the reflexive cycle supporting your poor habits. When you detach from being pre-occupied with all things that are you, there is a neurological, chemical and therefore physical effect that cannot support or feed your current habits.

Step 3

Compose Yourself

How it Works

With 2-3 blank sheets of paper, begin writing as fast as you can whatever is in your head. DO NOT judge, worry about grammar, punctuation, legibility or try to make it about anything specific. This is a free flow, subconscious mind dump, from your head to paper. Curse, be profane, prolific, happy, angry, sad or silly. Let whatever is in you flow uninterrupted from pen to paper. Feel free to begin by writing how weird you think this exercise is. What you write does not need to make sense, and might look or feel like inane ramblings - it's all good! When finished, shred or file your writing and move on with your day.

Although you can **Compose Yourself** anytime, it has a more profound impact immediately after waking in the morning, before you interface with any person or technology. This means before email, phone or TV. You heard me, BEFORE email or phone. Close your eyes and take a breath - you can do it! The point is to start your day by creating reflexive subconscious behaviors that support your goals, while disempowering reflexive habits that oppose your efforts.

Why it Works

This is a daily, subconscious house cleaning, that first brings awareness, and then helps loosen and remove the harmful deposits in your subconscious mind. These damaging deposits create and reinforce habits that contribute to poor performance. This is an important dynamic, as the conscious mind references the subconscious mind for most of our *conscious actions*.

Our past and current Thoughts, Words and Actions are deposited in the subconscious mind. These deposits are reflexively used to shape our future Thoughts, Words and Actions. Much like a checking account, whatever deposits have been made, are what is available for withdrawal.

Remember, in this chapter, my objective is to quickly show you how **The Reflex** works, so you have the option of using it right away, without having to read the entire book. More detailed explanations and alternative ways to **Compose Yourself** can be found in later chapters.

Let's Review

THE REFLEX

1. Check Your Mind

2. Acts of Compassion

3. Compose Yourself

Check Your Mind to discover what you think and feel about your action/reaction regarding any circumstance or interaction with another living creature. Does your discovery support or oppose your **Guiding Principle**? There will always be times when it is the right answer to oppose your **Guiding Principle**, such as allowing yourself a small, frivolous purchase after six, unbroken months of diligently sticking to your goal of *spending less* and *saving more*. As long as you honestly feel good about your Thoughts, Words and Actions, in context of your Guiding Principle, you will continue to reinforce habits that support your goals.

Remember, alignment between your Thoughts, Words, Actions and **Guiding Principle** is crucial to your success. Therefore, if you **Check Your Mind** and do not like how you feel, name the thought or feeling you would like to replace it with and Perform some action that supports and expresses that thought or feeling. Consider that every Thought, Word and Action either supports or opposes your objectives.

Acts of Compassion. What is one small act you can perform that is for the benefit of another living creature? A kind act or thought is all this requires. Physically help someone, silently wish someone well or simply make eye contact, smile and say hello to a stranger as you pass by.

Compose Yourself. With 2-3 blank sheets of paper, begin writing as fast as you can whatever is in your head. DO NOT judge, worry about grammar, punctuation, legibility or try to make it about anything specific. This is a free flow, subconscious mind dump, from your head to paper.

Well my friends, that's it! Time to make a decision. Either jump right in and start integrating **The Reflex** into your life, or keep reading to gain a deeper understanding of its principles and applications.

Chapter 2

Guiding Principles

I believe in the power of **Guiding Principles** supported by daily ritual or process. Being grounded in a set of principles provides the footing required to successfully navigate a path towards a personally meaningful life.

In the previous chapter, we learned it is important to establish value driven, **Guiding Principles**, which enable you to create Thoughts, Words and Actions to reinforce those principles in support of your goals. In this chapter, we will more fully explore the nature and application of **Guiding Principles**.

Principles are what you believe and put your faith in. They provide a lens to focus and express your actions through. Principles shape how you perceive yourself, other people, circumstances and the world around you.

Personally, I visualize driving a stake or flag in the ground to represent my principles. This imagery creates a fixed point of reference in my mind and heart that anchors Thoughts, Words and Actions to support those principles.

In Chapter 1, I shared one of my **Guiding Principles, The** *thing* **Has No Power - You Do!** Another of mine is simply, *How can I help you?* With this basic sentiment, I have perfectly aligned both my principle and intent. This is important, as it makes it much more likely that my Thoughts, Words and Actions will support my end goals.

As the new host of the Tonight Show, Jimmy Fallon's first guest was former rapper turned movie star, Will Smith. While speaking on the topic of values and raising children, Will revealed that he tells his children "*... it is their job to use their minds and hearts to help others.*" Will continued by explaining that his family is guided by a principle to entertain for the benefit of others, rather than for their own ego.

Whether an entertainer, plumber, priest, rabbi, attorney, physician, teacher, writer, or stay at home parent, *how* you do what you do reveals your intent, and determines the quality of your expressed Thoughts, Words and Actions.

Don't Waste My Time

Six years ago, I came across a store on eBay with its sales page that read, *Don't waste my time with stupid questions. Only want fast sales.* Where to shop and who to buy from online is sometimes a process of elimination, and this person's principles made it easy for me to permanently cross his store off my list.

Although I don't agree with it, and wouldn't call it *principled*, this eBay shop owner does have a **Guiding Principle.** In my opinion, he simply wants people to purchase his products, with him investing as little effort as possible to capture the sale. His customer service appears to be limited to receiving your order, your payment, and shipping your item - done.

Intention

Guiding Principles are driven by purposeful intention. Without it, you are detached from what you feel and believe in your heart - your Authentic Self. When you struggle with your Thoughts, Words and Actions, it is because you have not established a **Guiding Principle** to plug your purposeful intent into. As a result, you will likely fail at your goals and resolutions, as you are subject to whatever reflexive responses are tied to your existing habits and behaviors.

The problem with principles and actions is the same issue that is often at the root of legal matters - intent. I feel comfortable concluding the eBay shop owner's service principles are not supported by an intent to benefit his customers beyond shipping the items they paid for. My impression is that he is much more interested in getting his personal wants and needs met, rather than his customers. I am reminded of Kevin Smith's first movie Clerks, where a video store employee says, *this job would be great if it wasn't for the f'ing customers.*

Buddhists use the term *Self-Grasping,* to describe the dynamic where we cling tightly to our ego driven, self-involved preoccupation with personal wants and needs, when they are not balanced by an intent to also help benefit others. The nature of *Self-Grasping* blurs our ability to see other people's needs and how we might help them. Yet, this belief does not diminish the importance of personal wants and needs, as it is understood we must also give to ourselves to be in a position to give to others.

So how do we resolve giving to ourselves, while also giving to others?

The distinction is marked by the power of one's intention, as our intentions dictate the words we choose, how we act and the choices we make. Giving to yourself so you are better equipped to help others, versus giving to yourself, with no intent to help others, changes how you express yourself, and that difference is perceived and felt by others.

This process is often seen during live entertainment. The audience is there by choice to be entertained - receive. The extent to which the performer engages with or gives to the audience, is often proportional to how much the audience engages or gives back to the performer. This dynamic becomes a powerful, reciprocating exchange of give and take, as the performer and audience feed on each other's energy, towards their mutual benefit.

Next, let's look at two physicians, Alex and Shane. Both are age 45, married and each have 2 children. Whether at personal or professional gatherings, Alex never misses an opportunity to let others know *I went to Harvard Medical School.* Alex exerts a fair amount of effort managing conversations to ensure you are as impressed with Alex as Alex is. Clients and friends alike are mostly props or supporting cast members for *The Alex Show.*

Meanwhile, unless you ask, you won't know that Shane also went to Harvard Medical School, as Shane is focused on learning about the other people in the conversation. Shane is searching for an opportunity to add value to the exchange, for their mutual benefit. Alex and Shane's conversations *feel* very different to both those observing and directly involved.

This difference between Alex and Shane's intentions generates specific Thoughts, Words and Actions that are deposited in the subconscious, which nourish, grow and reinforce each of their intentions - a crucial distinction. No different than the rest of us, the effects of Alex and Shane's intentions have a ripple effect that touches every other part of their lives - for better or worse.

Having spent the majority of my career as a fitness trainer and athletic development specialist, means I have spent the bulk of my time as a personal service provider.

Also included as personal service providers are physicians, attorneys, accountants, educators, massage therapists, coaches, trainers, painters, photographers, interior designers, house cleaners, wait staff, and personal stylists. Yet, for all the different occupations that exist in the personal service industry, there are only 2 ways for anyone to provide service. I either serve my needs first or your needs first. My choice is determined by my intention. If my intention is *How can I help you*, my focus in on you and how to best serve your needs.

Authentic Self

Guiding Principles are often an extension of one's Authentic Self. For this reason, it is important to discover as much as you can about the nature of who you are. This will help assure your **Guiding Principles** are in alignment with your Authentic Self and support your goals.

Although discovering your Authentic Self can be one of the most difficult tasks to undertake, it can also be the most rewarding and enlightening. After all, this is about YOU. Being honest in truly understanding yourself, is how you avoid years of trying to achieve goals and extract happiness from things, people and experiences that are not in alignment with who you truly are. Figure out if you are mostly defined by what the marketplace says and your consumer habits.

Discovering your Authentic Self requires you strip away as much societal and environmental conditioning as possible. Once you strip away the influences of religion, politics, school, upbringing, peer influence, marketing and advertising - who is left? What does that person independently think, feel and believe. This process may seem paradoxical, as many believe much of who you are is a by-product of all of these aforementioned elements. Strip those away and one could conclude there is no YOU left.

I disagree. These influences are not necessarily the root, core or foundation of who you are, but layered on top of and comingled with your Authentic Self. They merely represent your current mental, physical and emotional wardrobe. If you truly want to succeed in goals that improve your performance and happiness in life, then it is time to do a thorough assessment of your *wardrobe* to see what actually fits, expresses and represents your Authentic Self.

There is much research and many examples of siblings brought up with the same parental, environmental, experiential and socioeconomic conditioning, yet live by a vastly different code and set of **Guiding Principles** from one another. From this, they develop Thoughts, Words and Actions that plot dissimilar lifestyle trajectories, which either support or oppose a personally meaningful, happy life.

If you are five foot, five inches tall, and have limited eye-hand coordination, with no ability to jump or run well, you will never become a professional basketball player. Spending your life reading, watching and playing basketball, will not change this.

Immersing yourself in their world by traveling, practicing, and living with the team, thereby having most of your experiences and frames of references greatly influenced by professional basketball players, still will not change your physiological and biomechanical template, or the reality that you will not play professional basketball.

The same is true for our mental and emotional hardwiring. Yes, these systems are flexible and can adapt, but only within their hardwired, genetically predisposed capacity.

Regarding relationships, academics, occupation or sport, no matter how hard you work at something, there will always be others who can work far less, while achieving far more due to differences in capacity.

Check Your Mind, to determine if you feel my words above are pessimistic or optimistic, limiting or liberating.

There is an empowering liberation that goes along with honestly identifying your Authentic Self, divorced from what advertising, magazines, social media, talk shows, your peers and special interest groups (political, religious, etc) tell us how we should look, act, speak, dress, like, dislike and live.

When you discover your Authentic Self, you will be assured of creating a **Guiding Principle** that will enable you to align your Thoughts, Words and Actions in support of your goals and happiness.

On the other hand, if you choose not to examine your life to discover the difference between your conditioned self and Authentic Self, then it is likely that from your perspective, the two will become indistinguishable from one another, and your ignorance may or may not be bliss.

What Orbits in Your Solar System?

A **Guiding Principle** is vital to performance, success and happiness, as it is a fixed reference point in your heart and mind that guides you from moment to moment towards your destination. Much like the relationship between our sun and the revolving planets in its solar system, **Guiding Principles** have a gravitational pull, which attract Thoughts, Words, Actions, people, circumstances, habits and behaviors, which support and reinforce the qualities and values of the principle.

Good or bad, whatever your principles have attracted, become suspended in orbit around you where they strengthen each others position. As a result, they are your reflexive point of reference, and orientation for your future Thoughts, Words and Actions. This by the way, is the process by which all habits are created.

Having your first child is an example of a fixed point in one's life. Most people take this opportunity to define principles of how they will act as parents and guide their child's development.

The nature of a child, to be dependent on others to survive, when aligned with the parent's **Guiding Principles,** automatically attracts a lifestyle in the form of Thoughts, Words and Actions, which support their **Guiding Principles,** while at the same time eliminating things that oppose these values. It then follows, we begin to struggle when we do not have practices in place to help create Thoughts, Words and Actions that align with our principles.

Do I Have a Gender Bias?

We could probably come up with some pretty colorful examples of the kinds of people and circumstances the guy from my eBay story would attract with his egocentric principles. As well, we could draw a few valid conclusions about the people and circumstances that would be drawn to a store that has strong customer service values.

As I reread the previous paragraph, I **Checked My Mind** and discovered I felt a bit conflicted referring to the eBay store owner as *the guy*. Why did I reflexively assume the eBay store owner is male? Perhaps I should simply shrug it off as a colloquialism, or a widely accepted, gender neutral phrase such as *you guys* or *mankind*.

The problem is that these reasons are not valid - for me. I assigned a gender to this person, because at no point while on that eBay store webpage, or while relaying the story to you in this book, did I ever picture anyone else other than a man. Frankly, I could not imagine a woman writing those words and expressing that kind of attitude to her customers. Perhaps my imagination is limited in this respect.

If we surveyed 10,000 people, I would expect the overwhelming majority would conclude the person who wrote that eBay web page is male. Regardless of the outcome of such a survey, I am still left to determine how I personally think and feel in context of my **Guiding Principles**, divorced as much as possible from external influences or conditioning.

Does my reflexive gender bias help support or oppose the creation of Thoughts, Words and Actions that aid me in helping others? If my objective is to help people, then I feel my mind should be as open, flexible and as least judgmental as possible.

So I **Checked My Mind** and discovered I did not like the way I thought or felt about my assumption on gender. Chewing on minutia? Perhaps. However, if your objective is to improve the quality of your life, I suggest you develop a bit of an appetite for minutia, as that is what the subconscious chews on 24 hours a day, whether asleep or awake. *The devil is in the details and so is happiness.*

In addition to reinforcing the alignment between my **Guiding Principles** and my Thoughts, Words and Actions, the power in putting my attention on this subtle, seemingly insignificant example about gender bias, is to remind me that a *non-effect* cannot exist. Whether we are consciously aware or not, every Thought, Word and Action is responsible for deposits that either strengthen or weaken the support of our **Guiding Principles**. However small, every experience is an opportunity to learn something about yourself. This discovery presents an opportunity to decide if you like that quality or if it benefits you, and change it if necessary.

Subconscious Jigsaw Puzzle

We can liken the minutia in our subconscious to the many pieces of a jigsaw puzzle. While each one by itself is trivial, when combined with other pieces, allows you to create one and only one specific image.

Only the puzzle pieces the manufacturer has deposited in the box are available for withdrawal, and will only allow you to create one image. The specific designation of each piece, its shape, size and color, *its nature* if you will, determines what it may be used for. So if your subconscious is filled with variously sized and shaped negative *puzzle pieces*, it is in their nature to support negative Thoughts, Words, Actions and outcomes.

My simple issue of gender assignment is important, as it enables me to reflect on how I see and relate to people, circumstances and the world around me. It provides another opportunity to expose and challenge the value of those deposits in my subconscious, which support my reflexive assignment of gender under certain conditions.

On the surface, the gender example may seem trivial and harmless, but these pathways can give rise to discrimination and negative stereotyping. I am not saying they are equal. They are however, all included in the circle of things that give way to judgment and bias, which help grease the slippery slope of prejudice and discrimination in all its forms, opposing my **Guiding Principles** and goals. Keep in mind, both the devil and happiness are in the details.

You see, both the conscious and subconscious minds use a lot of reference points in constructing the thoughts and images that give birth to our words and actions. The moment I assumed the eBay store owner was male, I began constructing a mental image of him in my mind.

I reflexively extract data deposited in my subconscious from my experiences, conditioning and influence from my parents, school, friends, community, literature, movies, advertising and marketing.

From these reference points, I instantly create a picture that includes hair, face, body, clothing, speech pattern, and geographical location. I then take it one step further, and judge this person's value system, when in point of fact, I know virtually nothing about this person. See the slippery slope?

Yet, after all this activity and complex processing between my conscious and subconscious minds, the reality is that I do not know if this person is male or female, as there are no gender clues in the screen name or on the page. Put in perspective, it has taken you many minutes to read this story, and much longer for me to write it. However, from the time that I first read *Don't waste my time with stupid questions! Only want fast sales,* to my assigning gender and judging the character of this person, took but a few hundred milliseconds.

A few hundred milliseconds is less than one second, and brings us to the root of our why reflexive behaviors and habits are hard to change. Why is it easier for some people, at certain points in time, to make good or bad deposits and withdrawals between their subconscious and conscious minds? Why do we create Thoughts, Words and Actions that at times support our goals, while at other times oppose them?

I could bore us both with a lot of babble about neuroplasticity, cortical remapping and brain etching, all of which deal with the brain's ability to change and adapt through one's experiences. Sure, some of you would walk away feeling informed or think, *that's interesting*. However, I built **The Reflex** as a practical, not theoretical model, enabling you to take immediate action towards change. Appealing to recent research is limited and fleeting, as we can only cite research up to this point in time, the conclusions of which are guaranteed to change with the next wave of research.

No, we need something simple and unwavering. A core element that governs every action in our lives. We need an already accepted scientific rule, principle, or law, such as gravity, as these types of laws are what stand strong against the ever changing winds of research and marketing tactics. So, what is this scientific principle that is responsible for every Thought, Word and Action we create?

The answer is obvious...

ELECTRICITY!

Electricity?

That's right - Electricity!

The current that runs through **The Reflex** is the foundational principle of electricity. We run on electricity, and are alive because of electricity. Specifically, each heartbeat, every move we make and every thought we create, is a result of electro-chemical impulses.

Since our lives literally depend on electricity, do you think perhaps any rule that governs electricity might be important to us, especially when trying to modify behavior?

You better believe it is!

So what is this all important principle? What is the primary principle or rule of electricity? Think about this for a moment, most of you know this.

It always takes...

THE PATH OF LEAST RESISTANCE!

That's right; our bodies take the easiest, most efficient path available. Since we run on electricity, specifically, an electro-chemical communication network. our physical, mental and emotional processes are governed by *The Path of Least Resistance*.

So, the answer to the question of why we sometimes make good choices that support our efforts and goals, while at other times make poor choices that oppose our efforts is because...

It's Easier!

Don't confuse terms like *path of least resistance* and *easier* with something that is better or smarter. Even though your body reflexively takes the easy path, does not mean that path is best for you or your objectives. The most efficient path is not always the best. Since the body and mind communicate electro-chemically, they are simply tasked with receiving and responding to stimulation in the most efficient way possible, independent of any plans you may have. Sometimes this benefits you and your goals, and sometimes it does not. Ordering fast food through a drive-thru or grabbing a bag of pretzels is easier than making a nutrient dense meal, and a more efficient means to getting calories in your body, but is not the most efficient path to health and fitness. On a personal side note, I must remember there are times when the best application of my *Efficiency Principle* is to take the longer, more involved path.

The Path of Least Resistance

The path used most often puts up the least resistance. Each of our experiences and resulting Thoughts, Words and Actions, etch a neurological pathway in our brain. Our future Thoughts, Words and Actions, either reinforce or weaken this path and our reflexive use of it.

The following sequence of images illustrates an easy way to conceptualize The Path of Least Resistance.

Pictured here is a dense rainforest jungle with no established pathway. Carving a path here will require much time and effort to remove obstacles such as vines, plants, trees and rocks. This is a dynamic we initially experience in all areas of life that require development, including academics, sports, relationships, occupation and personal development.

As we repeat this process, we create a neurological pathway, which allows us to communicate our electro-chemical messages more quickly and efficiently. This pathway offers less resistance with repeated use.

This means, if you spend time practicing correct mathematical formulae, you will get better to some degree at math. And, if you spend time practicing incorrect mathematical formulae, you will get better to some degree at becoming worse in math.

Say What???

You see, we are designed to adapt, evolve and increase our capacity in the specific direction of the stimulation we receive. We either get better at doing something correct, productive, etc., or we get better at doing something incorrect, unproductive, etc. We don't get worse at things; we get better at doing things well and better at doing things poorly.

This by the way is how compensations in the body occur. We get better at overusing one part of our body, which leads to its breakdown, such as overuse injuries like carpal tunnel.

A drunk becomes better at drinking and better at demonstrating a lack of discipline and self control. Those who practice rude behavior get better at being rude, while those who practice compassion become better at being compassionate. A healthy mind and body does not devolve, but gets better at supporting either positive or negative behaviors, habits and development. *Practice makes perfect, we reap what we sow, we are what we eat...* you get the idea.

Regardless of which pathway we choose, correct/incorrect, productive/unproductive; the outcome is the result in having made that specific pathway, the Path of Least Resistance.

Similarly, when we practice poor nutrition, the mind and body adapt by making it easier for us to make poor food choices in the future. We get better at eating poorly. Now, replace poor nutrition with smoking, drinking, stress, procrastination, lying, productivity, passion, or motivation.

Perhaps you would like to break your habit of procrastination, as it increases your stress, while decreasing your productivity and efficiency at both work and home. Fortunately, an opportunity arises when your spouse asks you to do something. Immediately, you **Check Your Mind** to discover your first reflexive thought or feeling in response to your spouse's request. Regardless of whether your reflex was good or bad, it was the result of The Path of Least Resistance. Since you are following the steps of **The Reflex**, if your reflex was anything other than one that limits procrastination, take one of two action steps.

1. Remind yourself of your **Guiding Principle** and how your reflexive procrastination does not support it. Then, create new words to support your **Guiding Principle**, which reflect how you would like to reflexively respond the next time an opportunity arises. Now get up and perform the task you were asked to do.

2. The other option is to **Compose Yourself**. Both options enable you begin clearing a new Path of Least Resistance, which supports inhibiting procrastination. We will further explore **Composing Yourself** in chapter 6.

Once again, we find our efforts and success supported or opposed by our **Guiding Principles**, as they are values that can enable or disable.

Regarding procrastination, an example **Guiding Principle** could simply be *Family* or *Team Happiness*. You drive your *happiness stake* in the ground, to focus on the happiness of others. This develops an intent to consistently increase the happiness of others, which attracts Thoughts, Words and Actions that oppose your procrastination reflex.

The Power of Guiding Principles

Alcoholics Anonymous, Weight Watchers, Crossfit, paleo, vegan and raw diets, along with many religions, political movements and organizations, are all examples of lifestyles anchored to **Guiding Principles**. Members of these groups are true believers; aggressive and uncompromising in pursuit of their sobriety, health, fitness, religion, politics, or other lifestyle ideal.

Yet, for as popular and meaningful as these lifestyles are to their followers, there is absolutely nothing special, unique or magical about any of their specific activities, with respect to effectiveness. Some of us need a support group to take action, while others are able to act independent of a group. There are no shortage of people who quit their addictions, lose weight, improve their health, get the fit body they want, and practice their faith and politics outside the structure of a group. About the same number of people succeed as fail at Weight Watchers, Jenny Craig, paleo, vegan, and raw diets. Yet each success hails their organization as the best. There are also members of every religion that will state their religious and spiritual needs are met by their specific brand of religion.

They are all right!

This could not be the case if there were only one true path to sobriety, spirituality, losing weight or getting fit and healthy. There is magic, but it is not in the rituals or activities specific to any one group. Rather, the magic comes from simply having a **Guiding Principle**, regardless of its nature. Good or bad, it is the **Guiding Principle** within each group that gives rise to a lifestyle true believers can sink their teeth into, as they get swept up and empowered by something larger than themselves.

A lifestyle choice is synonymous with a **Guiding Principle**. Whether you have chosen an addiction recovery, diet, exercise, religious or political group, you have chosen a lifestyle anchored to the **Guiding Principle** of that group. This **Guiding Principle** becomes the sun in your lifestyle solar system, attracting to its orbit Thoughts, Words and Actions to support its ends.

However, the effectiveness of these groups is NOT due to having found the *right* or *correct* foods, diets, exercises or religious perspectives. The effect of buying into a paleo-diet **Guiding Principle,** means paleo-diet enthusiasts see the world through a paleo-diet lens. This influences where and how they shop, cook and eat, along with the logistics of their daily flow, as well as conversations with family and friends.

In turn, this places restrictions on certain Thoughts, Words and Actions, while enabling others.

Making the **Guiding Principles** of a paleo lifestyle central to their lives, enables them to make the subtle changes and course corrections that create habits necessary to achieve their health and fitness goals. As I stated earlier, there are as many people who fail at paleo, but succeed at Weight Watchers or on their own, and vice-versa.

The *thing* Has No Power - You Do!

My objective here is to illustrate that the correctness or validity of a group's ideals is NOT relevant for its members to benefit. The paleo or caveman diet has its eating choices and lifestyle rooted in the mistaken belief that we should eat as our Paleolithic, pre-agrarian ancestors did, only consuming nuts, fruits (including seeds) and vegetables. This belief was supported by the incorrect notion that our ancestors were physiologically the same as modern man, yet survived without grain in their diets, while having low incidence of modern disease. This led to the erroneous conclusion that emulating their diet is the road to health and fitness nirvana.

As this thinking has become disproven, a more common practice is to align one's diet with the advent of when paleo-man began hunting and cooking, which allows for the inclusion of meat.

A strict paleo perspective is one that eschews most food produced through modern agriculture and farming, as Paleolithic man did not grow his own food this way, but rather fed off the land.

Archeologists, anthropologists, and biochemists agree modern man is quite different than Paleolithic man. Paleo stomachs, intestines, intestinal bacteria, teeth and therefore biochemistry were structured for eating fruits, plants and insects.

As we evolved, we learned to hunt animals for meat, clothing and protection, and never looked back. We went from having a much larger gut that was good for fermenting rough cellulose and carbohydrate to a much smaller gut and bigger brain. The advent of cooking also changed how and what we ate, as well as enabling us to efficiently extract more nutrients from our food. Regardless, the fact remains it is impossible to eat like paleo-man did, as many of the foods they consumed have not existed for thousands of years.

Nevertheless, their powerful belief structure has prompted a growing movement where paleo-enthusiasts spend considerable time and effort foraging for special foods to try and emulate the image in their minds of a paleo-lifestyle. In doing this, they simply make central in their lives, a **Guiding Principle** to eat as naturally as possible. That's the magic.

By placing their *attention* on an *intention* to support the **Guiding Principles** of the paleo-movement, they have created a paleo-lifestyle. This action creates a re-prioritization of how they allocate their current lifestyle resources. Thoughts, Words and Actions that support the **Guiding Principle** become high priority, while those that oppose are diminished.

A similar dynamic was seen in my parent's generation, where a young husband with a child on the way, sold his *bachelor-life* sports car, for both money, and to signify that his focus and priorities (**Guiding Principles**) have changed from one that puts himself first, to one that puts family first.

My objective is not to criticize paleo diets or any other lifestyle choice, but to uncover the true root elements that give rise to empowering Thoughts, Words and Actions - Establishing and Believing in **Guiding Principles**!

Whether or not we are consciously aware of it, whatever motivates us to do and take action in life is attached to a **Guiding Principle**. Even if that action is to do nothing, as that choice is supported by an internal belief. Keep in mind, drug addicts, thieves, murderers, rapists, mean girls and boys, as well as the unmotivated and uninspired, also have **Guiding Principles**. Whether *principled* or not, the Thoughts, Words and Actions your principles support, determines whether or not you travel a path of happiness, productivity and fulfillment.

Chapter 3

Check Your Mind

When I presented **The Reflex** to the good people at M&M Mars/Wrigley company, I began by apologizing to them for having an unavoidable, last minute conflict, which required me to leave 30 minutes early.

I said, *I understand this presentation was scheduled for 90 minutes, but something has just come up that is beyond my control, and requires me to leave 30 minutes early. I apologize. So, this 90 minute presentation will be cut back to only 60 minutes. Since we have a lot to cover, we need to jump right in and get started.*

I paused and then said, *Now I want each one of you to* **Check Your Mind** *to discover the very first thing you thought or felt when I told you I was leaving 30 minutes early. Not the second or third thought, but your very first reflex. Be honest, as there is no right or wrong answer.*

I went on to say, *How many of you immediately thought, (with fist pump)Yes! I get out of here 30 minutes early, and started filling in the time with things you could do? Perhaps get something to eat, check email, return phone calls, zone out, or get in a round of Angry Birds?*

Five people raised their hands, a few others nodded their heads in agreement and everyone had a good laugh. I thanked them for their honesty and asked my next question.

How many of you thought, Oh how unfortunate we're going to miss out on 30 minutes of what I'm sure will be an AMAZING and enlightening presentation? Again, everyone had a good laugh and to my surprise, 3 people raised their hands and I even heard one person say, *that's what I thought, I was looking forward to this.* I know it is popular to believe that every employee snoozes their way through seminars and can't wait to leave, but some people are truly interested in improving their quality of life, at work and home.

Next I asked, *So how many of you took a bit of a cynical position and thought, Well that was an awkward start dude, nice way to set the tone.* Again, three people raised their hands, and a woman replied, *that did seem weird.*

Finally, I asked, *did anybody take a compassionate route, thinking I hope everything is okay with him?* Two people raised their hands while I overheard a person say, *that never occurred to me*, along with a few that looked sheepishly at each other with wide eyes, shrugged shoulders and the "Oops" smirk we get when caught overlooking some small act of compassion or social etiquette.

Although I exposed everyone in attendance to the exact same circumstances, my leaving 30 minutes early, it was internalized and reflexively reacted to in many different ways. Whether the attendees were happy, disappointed, irritated, indifferent, inquisitive, or compassionate, was the result of the deposits made to their subconscious minds prior to entering that room. This colored how they viewed, interpreted and internalized the event, which contributed to each of their reflexive responses.

Think of **Checking Your Mind** as an accounting practice to discover the nature of your deposits. Only then can you decide if they support or oppose your goals, principles and happiness. **Checking Your Mind** is a self-discovery process that enables you to better understand your mind and heart.

What does it say about your character, mind, focus, level of interest, work ethic, or your perceived value of the event, if you are excited about any opportunity to leave early, especially when my exercise exposed people sitting next to you who feel the exact opposite sentiment? Many of us care about self-improvement, even at work.

Why are you there in the first place? Do you think this attitude or perspective helps or hinders your productivity, level of contribution or career trajectory? These are merely possible questions you could ask yourself after you **Check Your Mind**. Alternatively, it could be you were looking forward to the presentation, and are serious about your career, but feel obligated to get home as quickly as possible to care for your spouse or child who is home sick. This is why there is typically not a universal right or wrong when you **Check Your Mind,** only right or wrong for you, in context of your principles, value system and life. Therefore, it is important you are honest about what you think and feel when you **Check Your Mind**.

This is also why it is vital to align what you *think* with what you *feel*, as it is far too easy for the mind to reflexively rationalize poor choices. This is typically expressed by thinking one way, yet feeling another, so your actions do not support your thoughts. The resulting effect is reinforcement of poor habits, which will oppose your future efforts. For example, your head says exercise today, but you simply don't feel like it, so you feed your head a justification to try and make yourself feel better about not exercising.

Checking how you *feel,* synonymous with **Checking Your Mind,** provides feedback as to whether or not you are making excuses and intellectual justifications in support of poor choices. This process enables you to clearly and honestly see if your Thoughts, Words and Actions support or oppose your **Guiding Principles** and goals.

Food doesn't make you fat or unhealthy, poor habits do!

The friction that many of us feel when trying to improve ourselves in any area of life is often due to our subconscious and conscious minds being out of alignment. If the goal in my conscious mind is to lose weight, yet my subconscious is filled with deposits that support a poor attitude towards nutrition and exercise, then my best case scenario is to struggle my way through a miserable process, which I probably won't maintain to see long term results. Most likely scenario, I will put some effort into the process for a few weeks/months and then quit.

When you **Check Your Mind** regarding weight loss, you have an opportunity to align your conscious and subconscious minds through honest, self-discovery. This illuminates the division line between what we *think* and what we *feel*, a line that is often blurred and hard to distinguish.

This incongruity between what we *think* and *feel* is often at the core of why we fall short of fulfilling our goals and meeting our objectives. My mind or intellect, might buy into the idea of weight loss because I'm a well educated, enlightened person, whose peers also value this quality. In addition, much of Hollywood and the media values it, and I am conditioned through marketing and advertising to *think* this is important. So looking thin or fit, has high *Social Currency*. Therefore, this is what I *should* be doing, not necessarily *Feel Like* doing. We struggle when what we *think* is not in alignment with what we *feel*.

Emotion Creates *Motion*

Buddhists say that change and fulfillment only occurs when we move what we think from the level of our head down to our heart. The idea may start in the mind, but until it is mixed with your heart, your emotions, how you feel, it lacks the required power to create meaningful, lasting change or fulfillment. Said another way, *emotion creates motion.*

It is interesting to note that our society's weight and fitness compulsion is a recent phenomenon, as compared to our much longer history of associating high *Social Currency* with some girth, being overweight or being considered fat. Being well fed was seen as a sign of prosperity, or having success as a hunter, gatherer or provider. The term *Fat Cat* was used as recently as the mid 20th century to describe a wealthy or powerful person.

I *think* and *feel* that some of you might be curious as to why I often use weight loss in my examples. Why not stress, depression, addiction, occupation, education, productivity, or relationships? In our society, weight loss is always a hot topic with broad based coverage and exposure across all media channels. As our society is chronically image conscious, how one looks is a universal topic. Either you or someone you know, struggles with weight loss, body image and/or fitness.

On the other hand, we can also say this about stress and productivity. The difference is that weight loss is one of the few issues and personal goals that cannot be camouflaged or relegated only to the internal domain of your heart and mind, where your struggle cannot be seen by most other people. Unlike being overweight, these other issues are easier to hide from both yourself and others. Being overweight has both an internal and external component, of which the external cannot be hidden.

What about those who want to quit the habit of smoking? Isn't smoking an external process that cannot be hidden, similar to being overweight? Not exactly. We continue to confine smokers to areas where we see them less and less. In my daily travels, I rarely see anyone smoking. Even those who I know smoke, I seldom witness in the act of smoking.

So, I choose to use weight loss examples more frequently than others, because I see it as a topic that is more universally understood and accessible to help you apply **The Reflex**.

Communication

Communicating through spoken or written words is one of the most ideal times to **Check Your Mind**. It takes a bit of practice, but is extremely effective at steering your conversation in real time, towards mutual satisfaction. It is an engaging and empowering process of checks and balances that enables you to keep in alignment your feelings, Thoughts, Words, Actions and **Guiding Principles**.

Like most good practices, positive outcomes begin with preparation. So, **Check Your Mind** before you engage with the person(s). This is your opportunity to expose whatever subconscious triggers, baggage or expectations that may give rise to Thoughts, Words and Actions that oppose your **Guiding Principles** and a productive outcome.

Now that you have prepped your mind and heart, **Checking Your Mind** during a conversation, will disable, or interfere with, securing a defensive position or thinking you know what the other person is going to say, while in reality, misunderstanding their intent. This often happens with those we have relationships with - personal or professional. There is a history that we use to color the words and messages we receive, which can reflexively bias our responses.

Checking Your Mind enables you to more closely listen and accurately hear what the other person is saying, while keeping your mind and heart open. In essence, you become more available and accessible to the person you are communicating with. This creates the causes for everyone to benefit. Remember, everything we do affects everything else - it's all connected. A positive or negative conversation will carry forward and impact your Thoughts, Words and Actions in your upcoming personal and professional interactions. Whether seconds, minutes, hours or days later, the laws of cause and effect are always in play. There cannot be a non-effect. How you communicate in one instance influences how you communicate the next, as well as how much emotional reserve you are able to carry forward.

Chapter 4

Deposits and Withdrawals

The conscious mind references the subconscious mind to produce the majority of one's Thoughts, Words and Actions. Good or bad, whatever you have deposited into your subconscious mind, is what is available for the conscious mind to withdraw.

Understanding that the relationship between the conscious and subconscious mind is dependent on a system of Deposits and Withdrawals, helps demystify the interplay between these parts of the brain. Similar to a checking account, the funds available for withdrawal are dependent on the funds that have been deposited.

Going deeper into this concept, we can make various types of deposits to a bank account such as cash, checks, electronic, and have those deposits reflected as checking, savings, money market and certificates of deposit.

If my goal is to make purchases by writing checks or using my debit card against my checking account, yet I only deposit money into my savings account, then my deposits will not support my efforts to withdraw funds, and I will fall short of my goal. My Deposits and Withdrawals are out of alignment, as I can only write checks or make debit card purchases against my checking accounts, which I have not funded. As soon as I realign my accounts, by making deposits to my checking account, my goal of making purchases with check or debit card becomes possible.

Our Thoughts, Words and Actions are the currency we use to make Deposits and Withdrawals to our subconscious and conscious minds. If I spend my day focusing on myself, my wants and needs, to the exclusion and at the expense of other people, those are the types of deposits that will be reflected on my subconscious balance sheet. Therefore, what is available for my conscious mind to withdraw, in constructing my Thoughts, Words and Actions, are limited to those that are mainly self-serving.

Reality Check. We all need to carve out time to focus solely on ourselves, as long as it is offset by deposits that also focus our attention on helping other people. Even better, use the power of intention in situations where you give to yourself, to help others. For example, I feel mentally, emotionally and physically better after going to the spa. As a result, I have greater internal resources to help others. I am mindful before, during and after the spa treatment, that the benefits I receive enable me to benefit others.

How We Drive Exposes The Mind and Heart

I drive to many of my appointments throughout the week, and discovered a long time ago that our driving habits, and responses to other's driving habits, reveal a great deal about what we carry in the mind and heart.

I'll share a story about merging on the highway, that some of you will be able to relate to in a general way. About 5 years ago while driving on the Kennedy Expressway in Chicago, I cross over into the off-ramp lane as I intend to exit. This off-ramp lane is about a quarter mile long and is shared by traffic that is both merging on and off the expressway. There are about 10 car lengths between myself and the car that is merging on. This driver accelerates and attempts to merge in front of me to my right, even though I am exiting and he needs to merge on the expressway in the next lane to our left.

As the merge lane is a single lane, there isn't room for him to accomplish this, so he quickly applies his brakes for a second, then lurches forward as if he is going to hit the side of my vehicle by aggressively and repeatedly, accelerating and braking. Perhaps he was hoping my reflex would be to apply my brakes for fear of him hitting me, and in doing so would provide an opportunity for him to accelerate in front of me. Instead, my reflex was to do nothing but maintain my speed, which prevented him from passing.

My exact thought was, *the last thing I want is this guy driving in front of me. He's an accident waiting to happen and if he's behind me, I don't have to worry about him as much.*

I am watching this same driver who is now behind me, as he cuts off a driver in the expressway lane next to me in a last ditch effort to pull along my driver's side and communicate with me before I exit. Since his convertible top is down, I can clearly see him shaking his thumb at himself as he yells, *YOU GET BEHIND ME!* With barely enough time before exiting, I look at him, laugh, shake my head and state the obvious, *Apparently not.*

Sometimes it is difficult to correctly understand someone's intent, what is in their heart and mind. Yet, I think it is fair for me to conclude that this driver was not making deposits to his subconscious that will support positive Thoughts, Words and Actions. As such, I believe his words and actions revealed the nature of the existing deposits that were available for his withdrawal. To quote philosopher John Locke, *The actions of men are the best interpreters of their thoughts.*

I could go further and say this driver was displaying a zero sum game mentality, as every driver he passed or cut off is someone he "won" against. However, Buddhists would say, is this assessment on *my mind's side* or *his mind's side*? Meaning, is it him or me? Do I have negative or biased deposits in my subconscious which colored how I perceived his intent?

In all honesty, when I **Check My Mind**, I can tell you that I did judge him to be "One of those drivers..." whose only objective while merging, is to cut off as many people as possible to get as far in front of the line as possible.

Whether I judged this driver fairly or not, I am left with two questions I need to answer for myself - *why did it matter to me*, and *were my Thoughts, Words and Actions in alignment with my* **Guiding Principles**? Part of me did not feel as his actions obligated me to do anything, so I kept my present speed and whether he passed me or not, so be it.

One thin layer beneath this however, exposed the truth. I reflexively decided the guy was an ass, and wanted to deny him the satisfaction of cutting me off. Now, I can rationalize that there is nothing wrong with me hoping someone who is acting like a fool, is met with the natural consequences of his actions. However, as I continued to **Check My Mind**, I needed to know why there are times under similar circumstances, when I feel those are opportunities to help someone achieve something that is important to them (without judging them), versus this incident, where I judged him and did not *Feel Like* being flexible or accomodating. The answer is that sometimes my subconscious account is flush with deposits that support more compassionate reflexes, while at other times it is low on funds or simply overdrawn.

Compassion

I shared this story to illustrate that every moment is an opportunity to decide what kind of deposits you will make to your subconscious mind. It is these deposits that will determine how you reflexively respond the next time. The key is to generate these deposits through kindness and **Acts of Compassion.**

To achieve this in meaningful areas of your life requires making more deposits than not, which support the desired reflexive response. Start by identifying an example in your life where you would like to reflexively respond in a different way. A reflex that supports, rather than opposes your goals, well being, happiness and **Guiding Principles.**

Checking Your Mind and **Composing Yourself** prepares the path, enabling you to efficiently deliver a behavior changing and performance enhancing elixir - **Compassion.**

When I have made deposits from compassionate Thoughts, Words and Actions, I feel a greater awareness of others needs, along with a desire to be more accommodating, empathetic, emotionally generous and helpful. Getting cut off while driving in this frame of mind, enables me to genuinely smile, feel compassion and express that compassion, by wishing the person well. Typically I will smile and say, *go for it, you must need this. Hope your day gets better pal.*

Cha-Ching! Not only does my response feel great, but also made powerful deposits to my subconscious mind, that are available for immediate withdrawal. Said another way, compassionate deposits make it easier to be compassionate the next time an opportunity presents itself.

The Devil is in The Details - So is Happiness

Whatever one does, should be done thoroughly - details are important. It is the little things we say, do or omit, that either binds together our larger actions or dissolves them.
I bring this up to address why I am specifically not discussing, or giving examples of *Big, Heavy, Life Issues,* such as love, infidelity, divorce, changing careers and so forth. These are all by products of many smaller decisions, with details that are easy to ignore or perceive as mundane.

The fact is, most of our *Big* issues in life are created from, and the product of, tens to thousands of smaller decisions. Those decisions are the end result of our Thoughts, Words and Actions, forged from the deposits made to the subconscious mind. In turn, this establishes what is available for the conscious mind to withdraw when making decisions.

Marriage, divorce, children, adoption, what college to attend, which occupation, or what home to buy, is not a singular decision. Rather, it is the end result of many decisions daisy-chained together, which over time leads you to your end decision.

When we explore these smaller details we learn where our true power for behavioral change, performance and happiness comes from.

With this in mind, I will share one more mundane, personal experience, to illuminate how any situation that occurs in your life can be used to make deposits that align with your **Guiding Principles**, and change your reflex.

Miele

Miele (pronounced mee-luh) is a German manufacturer, which among other household appliances, makes vacuum cleaners. Loosely translated from German, Miele means, *You paid way too much for that vacuum.* I discovered this when my wife replaced our Oreck vacuum with a Miele. I seriously had no idea you could spend that much on a vacuum cleaner. To be fair, it does its job, it *sucks*, but I did not think it *sucked* that much better to justify the difference in price. Provided the vacuum was returned in saleable condition, we had 30 days to test it at home. When I suggested to my wife that she should consider returning it, she said, *I would, except it now has two large scratches.*

An odd thing happened next. As I realized we must now keep this overpriced, cosmetically damaged vacuum, I began to feel a bit protective towards it. I saw it as an investment to dollar cost average down over the course of its life. The longer it lasts, the better I feel about it. Strange? Perhaps. Regardless, it set the stage for what happened next.

Two days later, I hear a crash as an object falls on the hardwood floor, and hear my wife exclaim, *Whoa, that was close!* I quickly poke my head out of the room I am in and see my wife pick up the vacuum from its side lying position, where it had fallen on the floor over her feet. It takes about 300 milliseconds for me to form a conclusion and say, *Ugh, did it break?!*

My wife looks at the vacuum, then quizzically at me for a moment, cocks her head and says, *No, it's not broken, but my foot is fine, thanks for asking.* Oops - major red face!

I literally winced inside, as I became painfully aware of a truth I exposed about myself I was not proud of. Whenever my wife hears an object fall on the floor, her reflex is to ask, *Is everyone okay?* She checks on the health of the *person first*. By contrast, I check on the health of the *object first*. So, I **Checked My Mind** to discover how I thought and felt about my reflex. First, I went through a logical justification to support my reaction. However, in the final analysis, I did not like how I felt and wanted to emulate my wife's reflexive response.

You see, my reflex that checks on the health of the object first, didn't feel right because it was not aligned with my **Guiding Principle** - *How can I help you?* A few minutes later, I had another realization. Due to the sarcastic nature of my family, they would get a lot of mileage out of my reaction.

What should I do now?

I had experienced a common life event that was not my first, and honestly, will not be my last - an inconsiderate, reflexive response to someone. In this case, my wife.

1. I **Checked My Mind** and discovered I didn't like what I thought or how I felt.

2. I did not like the way I felt, because my reaction was not aligned with my **Guiding Principle** - to help others.

At this point I have gained awareness of a reflexive behavior I would like to change, *checking the health of the object first*, and identified a replacement reflex, *checking the health of the person first*, as the rest of my family does. Now What? Although **Checking My Mind** has revealed a misalignment between my **Guiding Principle,** and my Thoughts, Words and Actions, it does not necessarily provide me with a tangible next step. I need an action step that bridges the gap between **Checking My Mind** and a creating a change in my reflexive responses.

This is where the magic happens...

Chapter 5

Acts of Compassion

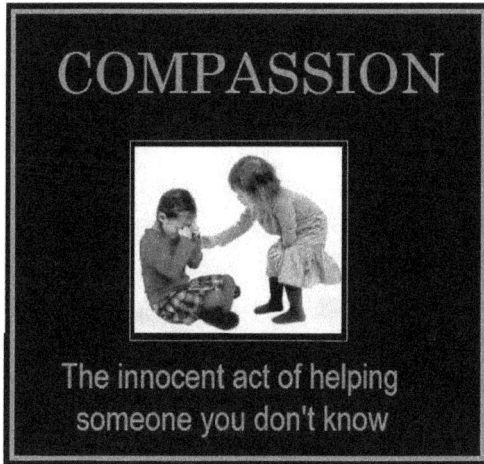

COMPASSION

The innocent act of helping
someone you don't know

Give to others to give to yourself. It truly is that simple.

William James said, *It is impossible to think of someone in a rage without at the same time envisioning them prone to vigorous action.* Essentially, the motion goes with the emotion. This is why the stress and anger off switch is a smile, as they are conflicting emotions that cannot simultaneously coexist. An **Act of Compassion** disrupts the cycle of your personal preoccupation, and redirects your attention to focus on the benefit of another sentient being.

Regarding the vacuum cleaner incident, **Checking My Mind** also revealed that I was feeling stressed. I stretched myself thin during this period of time, as I was concurrently developing and preparing for my first presentation of **The Reflex**, creating a new website in an unrelated field, running my offline training business, and writing a book on youth sports nutrition - Whew! Not surprisingly, the more stressed I became, the more difficult I found it to make progress and manage all my *spinning plates*. This in turn only served to produce more stress and inefficient work flow.

Since I was feeling *squeezed*, as my daughter would say, I did what many of us do and unloaded some of those negotiable *extras* in my life, including time spent with family, exercise, and proper nutrition. Interestingly, the nature of these *extras* are personally fulfilling, enriching, and therefore exactly what we need to help support us during times of stress, to most efficiently achieve our goals.

This common dynamic and deluded logic is similar to not taking time to get proper shoes to train for running a marathon, because that would take time away from training.

This became particularly clear the more I disengaged from **Composing Myself**, **Acts of Compassion** (by only focusing on my single minded task) and **Feeding My Body** (exercising less than once per week, not eating well and spending stretches of 6-12 hours without moving from my desk).

Essentially, I cut off the supply of what inhibits stress reduction and nourishes improved performance. The result of this only served to feed and strengthen those negative conditions, and the reflexive behaviors that oppose my goals.

Regardless of the specific circumstances involved, the question for each one of us when we find ourselves at these types of crossroads and wanting to change our behavior should be, *how do I realign with my* **Guiding Principles***?*

For myself, I had to realign with my objective to help others. I literally said to myself, *Dude, you're being a hypocrite, no wonder you're struggling. You're trying to help others apply tools you've stopped using right now. WTF are you doing?*

With an air of frustration, I pushed my keyboard out of the way, grabbed a few sheets of blank scrap paper and began to **Compose Myself**. I have a drawer in my office filled with discarded printer paper and mail that I use the blank side of for both scrap paper and **Composing Myself.**

This is the part of the story where I'm supposed to tell you I heard a chorus of angels sing, as everything snapped back into place for me and I was again struggle free. My actual experience turned out to be something less than awe-inspiring. Yet, it was real and necessary.

It was a struggle to **Compose Myself** for even one page. I was agitated and could not sit still, as my dominant reflex at the time was to reject everything that was not directly related to my projects.

While writing that single page, I felt the pull of my body and mind summoning me to stop wasting my time trying to **Compose Myself,** and get back to doing something relevant (I will address this dynamic in more detail shortly). Remember, this process is a subconscious mind dump, so this is exactly the kind of things that should be written down, and that is exactly what I did - for one page.

However, that one page was enough of an intervention to activate my reset button. I felt like I could breathe easier as if I had been gifted with a sense of composed clarity. I felt gratitude and performed a quick Buddhist dedication practice.

Dedications

This simply involves offering up your good fortune, blessings, well wishes for others, or your Thoughts, Words and Actions at that moment, to whomever or whatever you believe in, or simply making a general offering to a visual you have in mind of the world. *I offer up this feeling of calm, composed clarity and the opportunities it will bring.* This is followed by dedicating your good fortune and the good will you previously offered, for the benefit of specific people, including yourself and the world in general.

I dedicate this offering, my good fortune, to myself, my family and all sentient beings, so we may all experience good fortune and happiness. The point is not to covet your good fortune, but in your heart and mind, share it with the world by desiring it to also benefit those around you, which in turn continues to benefit yourself. Circle of life baby - It's all connected!

Fear Not! I am not trying to lead you down a religious path, Buddhist or otherwise, as I am grounded in faith and spirituality, not religion. I do however, encourage you to try *dedications,* or create your own meaningful process. Regardless of its origin, any practice, ritual or action you perform, that is predicated on both giving and receiving compassion, mindfulness and good fortune, will provide immense personal value to yourself and others.

Dedicating good fortune on any level is important to Buddhists, as they believe it magnifies the effects of good fortune, while diluting the effects of *Self Grasping.* This is a term Buddhists use to describe the act of clinging too tightly to one's actions, ego, self-importance, or possessions. Making *dedications* provides another opportunity for one to give, which creates the conditions to receive.

I am sharing my *dedication* practice to expose your mind to deeper levels of **The Reflex.** However, I did not include the practice of *dedications* as one of the steps in **The Reflex** model, as I thought it might make some people uncomfortable, or simply be too much to bite off and chew at one time, thereby creating a point of resistance - which would oppose my goal.

My expectation is that many of you will not incorporate a *dedication* practice, at first, and that is understandable and your choice. However, I will make the following deposit to your mind for your consideration.

Every Thought, Word and Action either supports or opposes your efforts in whatever is important to you. Every Thought, Word and Action has an effect, good or bad. They either create or reinforce something positive or negative, as the condition of a *non-effect* cannot exist. An act of *dedication* simply adds another reinforcing layer of support.

Personally, I believe one of the most powerful aspects of *dedications* is that it increases the time you spend in a compassionate space, focusing on Thoughts, Words and Actions that give to and help others, while reinforcing the alignment with your **Guiding Principles.**

Let's Recap

I **Composed Myself** for one page, and felt good. My intervention had disrupted my reflexive response and dissolved subconscious deposits that do not support my **Guiding Principle**. I dedicated that act and felt even better.

At this point, **The Reflex** required me to commit an **Act of Compassion** to bridge the gap between awareness and behavioral change. This enabled deposits to my subconscious, which would be available for withdrawal to support my **Guiding Principle**.

By merely placing my focus or *attention,* on the *intention* of committing an **Act of Compassion,** enabled me to begin looking outside of myself for an *object of my intention,* to place my *attention* on. This means looking for an opportunity to express compassion to someone or something.

Opportunity Knocks

Later that day, I was waiting at a stop light at the top of an expressway exit ramp. My attention was not inwardly focused, so I was consciously aware of my surroundings. I was not on the phone, or lost in my own self-involved thoughts, but rather, looking for my opportunity - an object of my intention to commit an **Act of Compassion.**

I noticed a person standing there, holding a sign that was asking for money. For reference, within a 10 mile radius of Chicago, there are people asking for money posted at many on/off ramp of our highways.

If you recall my *Efficiency Principle,* it should not surprise you that I rarely carry any cash or change - too cumbersome. This meant giving this person money was not an option. Instead, I looked at him in the eyes, smiled, and simply said, *Hi, I hope you have a nice day.* What happened next was imperceptible to anyone else, but an extremely powerful exchange between us. His eyes softened and opened wide. He stepped closer, lowered his sign and said, *Thank you, and God bless you.*

He did not ask for money, but merely stepped back as the light changed to green. As I drove away I silently wished him to have one more experience that day, which enabled him to smile and feel good.

That's it! That was my **Act of Compassion.** Nothing profound or grandiose, but rather a tiny, seemingly insignificant act of truly acknowledging a human being in that moment. While it is true that money would have helped him acquire some measure of food, clothing, shelter, or drugs, I'll wager that at that moment, he could not have felt richer or more internally fulfilled.

I **Checked My Mind** again, and discovered I felt thankful and empowered. In turn, this immediately changed how I looked at and felt about everything and everyone around me. Sit with that for a moment. Placing my *attention* on the *intention* of expressing an **Act of Compassion**, had the power to instantaneously change how I perceived everything. This experience immediately changed the lens I look at the world through, enabling me to perceive many richly layered colors and textures I normally pass by without notice. This is where our true power as human beings exists. The ability to change our reality, what we see, and how we see it, in any given moment - good or bad. I'm sure there was at least one person behind me at that stop light who looked at the same person I did, yet did so through a lens of negativity and judgment, or merely looked straight through him while feeling nothing.

At this point I was about 2 miles from home, so I directed my feelings and perspective towards my family, which positively impacted our interaction. All this, from having the courage and mindfulness to carve out a few moments of my time and exert a small amount of effort, to give to someone in a meaningful way. That's right, I said *Courage*. Think about it.

I'm sure many of you can appreciate the challenge and strain felt, while tearing yourself away from your vitally important, self-involved, personal business you must attend to while waiting at a stop light. Sarcasm aside, each of us can choose how we spend the gap between moments. A thoughtful pause before responding to someone increases the gap between the moment of action and reaction. The time spent waiting at a stop light, exemplifies longer gaps between the act of leaving point A and arriving at point B. These can be looked at as opportunities to reinforce an empowering or disempowering habit.

We can choose to reinforce our societal conditioning by filling every gap between moments in time, and deepen the bond with our mobile technology, or choose to make empowering deposits to our subconscious, through acts that enrich both the lives of others and ourselves.

I was thankful for the opportunity, and mindfulness to recognize, that someone other than myself had a need (literally in front of me). I felt fortunate I took action which added to his happiness, and after I drove off, that is exactly the *dedication* I made.

On the other hand, merely passing by someone on the street, saying *hey pal, have a great day*, while continuing to text, is not an especially meaningful expression of mindfulness or **Act of Compassion,** as you only placed a fraction of your *attention* on the object of your *intention*. Do you feel you have the full attention of the person you are speaking with who has their head down, with eyes and fingers glued to their phone?

Mindfulness

Mindfulness is being present and in the moment - aware. When you **Check Your Mind,** you are being Mindful. Putting your *attention* on your *intention*, or the object of your *intention*, requires you to release everything in your mind for a moment and only hold onto the object of your *intention*. It is in this space that you blend what is in your mind and heart, to see and feel your *intention*. Hint: In most cases you are not in a Mindful state if you have a mobile device in your hand.

My intention was to help another human being through an **Act of Compassion**. The object of my intention, was the man at the stop light. One way to understand this, is to visualize your thoughts or goals, which are at the level of your head, seep down to the level of your heart, and hold them there until you feel what was in your head. This action creates a powerful bridge between the head and heart, which enables us to *feel like* or *not feel like* carrying out our intentions and achieving our goals. We will thoroughly explore the powerful phenomenon of *feeling like* or *not feeling like* doing something in Chapter 8.

So, this one small, mundane event with the vacuum cleaner, provided an opportunity to completely change my reflex, reduce stress, become more efficient, and work less to produce more, which helped make my objectives so much easier to achieve. The secret to empowerment and lasting behavioral change, is believing that the way you choose to perceive, think and feel about anything, can determine what it becomes in the future. This is how we shape our reality.

Lifestyle Versus Acts of Compassion

The rest of this chapter uses varied examples to explore how society, our reflexive behaviors, and inwardly focused lifestyles, can interfere with expressing **Acts of Compassion**.

A few pages back I wrote, *While writing that single page, I felt the pull of my body and mind, summoning me to stop wasting my time trying to* **Compose Myself,** *and get back to doing something relevant (I will address this dynamic in more detail shortly).* Next we will explore this idea of *relevant actions* and how they affect our ability to commit **Acts of Compassion**.

Internal Support is Very Relevant

Taking the time to reflect, introspect, meditate, be mindful, compassionate, thoughtful and following the steps of **The Reflex**, are all examples of habits that internally support our ability to create empowering and life changing Thoughts, Words and Actions. Unfortunately, they also represent practices many of us feel we do not have time for.

Whether in personal or business life, *If it doesn't show, it doesn't go* is an often invoke concept. Sports coaches below the collegiate level are notorious for dismissing anything that doesn't look or *feel like* a sport specific action. Ignorance is bliss, as all that many of them know is to keep running plays and working skills and drills.

Even when presented with programs that develop the athlete's mobility, flexibility, stability, agility, strength, speed and power, which is what is needed to develop bodies and minds that can better apply those sport specific skills, many still think, *That's nice, but we've got real work to do over here.*

Important things, like overtraining, lack of proper recovery/adaptation cycles, only focusing on sport specific skills, which increase imbalances, while decreasing efficiency, and increasing the likelihood of acute and chronic injuries, while limiting performance and development. Whew! I agree, that will keep you and physical therapists quite busy.

Sports, Algebra, Your Home

In 2009 at a pre-season team parents meeting, I was explaining my athletic development program that was being incorporated into their competitive gymnastics program. I described exactly how the program would help the coaches develop their athlete's skills more efficiently, thereby building better gymnasts. The athletes would benefit from improved mobility, flexibility, stability, agility, strength, speed and power.

I also explained how this would help prevent many of their common injuries, as well as future aches and pains felt as adults, from youth sports programs that are coached by the old school principles of *more is better* and *use them up and wear them out.* I reinforced my program objectives with my **Guiding Principle** - *Powerful Athletes and Healthy Bodies For Life!* After I concluded my presentation, I opened the floor for questions. The first question, *How much time is this going to take away from training?* REALLY?! Take away from training? WOW!

It should not be viewed as a choice between this or that, but rather a necessary component to responsibly maximize development. How much time will running multiplication tables take away from learning *real* math? How much time will practicing algebra take away from learning calculus? In both cases, these are foundational components that are required to support the development of greater skill sets.

For most people, the value of learning algebra was not understood until presented with calculus, as algebra is a fundamental, structural support of calculus. Admit it. Some of you are thinking, *how come no one ever told us this about algebra?*

One could keep practicing calculus without a proper foundation in algebra, but for the majority, the depth of calculus skills developed would be quite limited. If we applied the typical youth sports model here, those who have less natural talent would simply practice more calculus drills, rather than develop a foundation to support calculus.

Similarly, many of us pay the least attention to the most important elements of our homes, including foundation, roof, electrical and plumbing. These parts sit there quietly in the background, providing support for every activity we enjoy in our home, relegated to their role as unsung heroes. We know they are vital because our lives are greatly disrupted when one or more of these systems does not function.

Although you may feel embarrassed and lose some *Social Currency* if your interior design aesthetics are off-putting to your guests, your house party can still proceed, largely unaffected. However, a leak in your roof, electricity goes out due to sub-par wiring, a water pipe bursts, or your basement takes on water due to cracks and an improperly sealed foundation, your party and most of the rest of your life comes to a screeching halt. A significant amount of your resources, including time, focus, effort and money, are immediately shifted to address these types of issues.

Stories from an electrician who has practiced in my community for the past 30 years, illuminates how some people struggle with this concept of internal support.

The median age of the homes in my zip code is 70 years, with others built between 1890-1920's. A famous architect greatly influenced the structure and design in this community. As such, tear downs are rare, while remodeling, restoration and preservation practices are always in full swing. As you can imagine, many of these homes are not fully up to electric or plumbing code.

During a conversation with the electrician, he told me kitchen fires are common due to faulty wiring. The interesting part is that most of these fires occur after the kitchen has had a $50,000 - $150,000 remodeling and appliance upgrade.

The electrician tells me, *people think nothing of paying $3000 for a warming drawer, but refuse to pay $5000 to properly bring their 70 year old wiring up to date, to support the added power consumption of modern appliances and lighting fixtures. The irony being, when their new kitchen is destroyed by the fire, they now need to pay $5000 or more to have me rewire anyway.*

As I said earlier, *If it doesn't show, it doesn't go.* You see, there is no *Self-Grasping* element to wiring or plumbing. It's hard to attach my ego to it, draw attention, or coax some praise or envy from you.

It is common practice in our culture to have a party or house walk to show off our newly remodeled homes and aesthetically pleasing things we have attached to our walls. However, we cannot do this with things in our walls, even though what is outside the walls is completely dependent on what is inside them.

Unfortunately, there are no bragging rights to me saying, *Check It Out!* I *rewired the entire kitchen. This bad boy is locked down with no electrical interference from any other part of the house. Got it sandboxed with its own separate breaker and dedicated lines to the power company's junction box.*

I didn't stop there, I also had the plumbing in all our bathroom showers replaced. Ripped out those spindly 3/8" pipes and installed 3/4". Turn on the faucet and it's like an F*!%#@g monsoon in here. Don't be shy, give it a test drive, there are towels in the closet.

Although this may require a shift in perspective, following the indirect path by taking time to develop internal support, is often the most efficient path to meet our objectives.

To be clear, this concept of *internal support*, and what is *inside the walls*, are metaphors for your heart and mind. I point this out in case anyone was thinking, *what does sports training, algebra and remodeling my house have to do with habits, behaviors, goals and happiness?*

At a corporate presentation of **The Reflex**, I told the Miele vacuum cleaner story and my encounter with the homeless person at the stop light (pg 73). A participant from the company's London office took a particularly literal interpretation by commenting, *well, I don't know of any homeless people where I live, so I don't see how this applies to me.*

I replied, *so your understanding is that in order to apply* **The Reflex**, *you need access to homeless people? Did anyone else get that from what I said?* If anyone else did, they did not own up to it. After the laughs faded, I not only rectified his misunderstanding, but also of others in attendance who may have felt similarly. The moral of the story, there will always be people who misunderstand you, as they color your words and actions with whatever is in their mind and heart.

This again is why it is so important to **Check Your Mind**, and discover the nature of the existing deposits that give rise to your Thoughts, Words and Actions. As discussed in the beginning of this book, this is also the process through which you will discover your Authentic Self.

Compassion is Strength

Another lesson learned here is that compassion is NOT being weak or passive. Stand up for yourself and others. Defend your position and territory. It is okay to draw a line in the sand and push back when being pushed. How you conduct yourself while doing this, the Thoughts, Words and Actions you choose, will be guided by your intention.

In my example on the previous page, when the person questioned whether they needed access to homeless people to commit **Acts of Compassion**, I reflexively reacted in three ways. First, I silently questioned whether he was being intentionally confrontational or simply not paying full attention, thereby hearing and understanding *homeless person* out of context. Second, I considered ignoring the comment. My third reaction was how I actually chose to respond. I **Checked My Mind** and felt I should respond from a place of compassionate strength. Doing this would help everyone in attendance more fully understand **The Reflex**, while providing me with another opportunity to personally apply my concepts in support of my **Guiding Principle** - *how can I help you?*

Regardless of this person's intention, I used his Thoughts, Words and Actions to put my *attention* on my *intention* of resolving any confusion, by making sure everyone understood the concept.

I share these personal stories to help illustrate how in any moment or situation, a few simple shifts in perspective and daily ritual, can have an amazingly profound impact on your success and happiness. Keep in mind what I wrote a few pages back, *The secret to empowerment and lasting behavioral change, is believing that the way you choose to perceive, think and feel about anything, can determine what it becomes in the future. This is how we shape our reality.*

Obfuscation (evasive, unclear, obscure)

One of the challenges we face today is that there are more layers, barriers, misdirection and confusing processes placed between us and our internal support network. This creates a disconnect between the heart (how we feel), mind and body, making it particularly difficult and foreign, yet as a result more necessary, to go through a process that enables you to discover the deposits you have made to your mind. This will enable you to uncover the quiet, subtle deposits made through the conditioning effects of society, which give rise to your Thoughts, Words and Actions. Remember, there cannot be a non-effect. The deposits made to the subconscious either support or oppose your goals and quality of life - period.

For thousands of years, our ancestors wore protective clothing or armor, along with available weapons, to protect themselves as they went off hunting and gathering. The armor and weapons were plainly visible and its purpose clear to all. Today, many of us start our day by putting on our figurative, less obvious suits of armor, as we prepare to go hunting and gathering (shopping), or enter the battlefields of school and work.

The armor and weapons we choose are much less obvious, as we don't literally put on a suit of armor or pick up a sword. Instead, we don whatever clothes and accessories we think reflect our *Social Currency*, grab our mobile tech weapon of choice, and get in the morning chow line, to fortify ourselves with a specialty coffee or energy drink before we head into the corporate or domestic battlefield for the day.

Like most things in our modern, homogenized, politically correct society, our Thoughts, Words and Actions aren't quite as clear and obvious as they once were. We have become too accustomed to accepting language and perspectives that have their edges softened, making them less precise and effective.

The word *Athleticism* is used liberally by the media, but it doesn't exist in the English language - yet. However, many of you are conditioned to accept this as a real word. One doesn't have *athleticism*, but rather displays athletic ability or talent.

Verizon and AT&T, along with the other mobile phone carriers use the term *subsidy* to describe the deal you get for not paying full retail price for your phone. In fact, this is an incorrect term as your phone is not subsidized.

For it to be a subsidy, the carrier would give you the phone for free, or sell it to you at a price below retail. Then a third party would pay the carrier the difference. In reality, the phone company often sells you a phone at a loss, using your monthly service payments (not a 3rd party) to make up the difference. They are simply giving you a discount on the phone in exchange for you agreeing to pay for one or two years of service.

Consider whether the legions of attorneys who work for these mobile phone carriers misunderstand the word *subsidy*, or whether the marketing gurus and behavior psychologists consulted, know exactly how the public has been conditioned to perceive the value friendly word *subsidy*, versus the proper industry term, Cost of Acquisition, their cost to acquire a customer.

Don't even get me started on the food industry and their Congress bedmates, redefining familiar terms on packaging and nutrition labels. If you think you know what you are buying - think again.*

---

*If you would like to find out the truth about food labels and ingredients, get my nutrition book **The 3/4 Rule** at Amazon.

Gone are the battle cries and unmasked, direct intentions of our armor wearing ancestors. Today we cloak our thoughts, words, feelings and actions, to maneuver or position ourselves within a consumer based paradigm, which honors acquisition over compassion or personal happiness. We continue to allow our personal happiness to be defined externally, and most often in context of consumption. The resulting problem is that many of us reflexively align our happiness with consumerism. This dynamic leads many to ask the questions...

Is this all there is? Is this what it's all about? Is this all I am?

We make it difficult to understand the true nature of our individual selves, and discover our personal path to a meaningful and happy life, when we allow obfuscation of our words, values and perceptions in the name of consumption. I encourage re-reading Orwell's chillingly prophetic book, *1984*. Each day, it seems his words become more relevant and reflective of our society's trajectory.

In our economy, corporate consolidation and the resulting duopolies and oligopolies are all the rage and our future. Nothing short of an alien takeover, complete economic meltdown, or the overwhelming majority of us deciding we will simply stop and live differently (my favorite option), is going to change this reality.

My point, regardless of circumstances, we all have the power to choose our **Guiding Principles** and value systems, which largely determines *HOW* we live and express ourselves. This is how we create Thoughts, Words and Actions to support more consistently committing **Acts of Compassion**. In exercising this power, we become the architects of our happiness, satisfaction and personal fulfillment.

The *thing* Has No Power - You Do!

Chapter 6

The Scripted Life

Yesterday, my daughter went on a rant questioning the purpose and values of society and life. *When we are little, we have a few great years when we are really happy. We can do what we feel like doing, not what society wants us to do. Then we have to go to school for the rest of our childhood, to prepare us to go to another school as adults, all so we can get a job. You can either work for yourself or someone else, and you may or may not make a ton of money. Regardless, what's the point?*

Developmentally, she is doing exactly what she should be doing, questioning the status quo, while finding her place in the world. Yet, if we slow down enough to increase the gap between one moment and the next, there is time to see a truth many of us are unaware of, or choose not to think about.

Like many people her age, my daughter sees the incongruity between what we have created to support consumerism and capitalism, and what we as human beings require to be happy and fulfilled - satisfaction derived through expression of the Authentic Self.

The difference lies in creating and consuming based on one's Authentic Self, versus creating and consuming based on how major corporations and legislators have helped shape and condition our needs and wants, in context of what it means to be happy. Rush Limbaugh built his career around his slogan, *Not sure what to think America? Don't worry, I'll tell you what to think.* Steve Jobs stated, *A lot of times people don't know what they want until you show it to them.*

This is seemingly a circular issue in that many businesses that sell directly to the consumer (as opposed to business to business), believe they offer products and services that reflect the expressed or perceived needs, wants and values of consumers and their society. The problem is that these values are typically not derived from the authentic selves of the population, but from their consumer selves, which have been conditioned to those wants. Many of us are like children raised on junk food or abuse. Since this is all we know and expect from the world, our Thoughts, Words, Actions, Needs and Wants are a by-product of, and serve to reinforce these conditions, habits and behaviors.

My daughter has taken the red pill,* unplugged, opened her eyes, and realized many of us are born into living a scripted life - as a consumer. It will be interesting to see how she responds to this reality over the next few years.

*In the movie The Matrix, the main character Neo is offered the choice between a red pill and a blue pill. The blue pill would allow him to remain in the fabricated reality of the Matrix, living the "illusion of ignorance", while the red pill would liberate him from the Matrix and into the real world, to live the "truth of reality". (Wikipedia).

D.M.S.

As a personal trainer for the past 20 years, I have had the opportunity to work with many stay at home moms whose professional degrees collect dust, but are fortunate enough to have the resources and a lifestyle that affords them the ability to live *the good life.* Still, many of them remain unhappy and unfulfilled.

I refer to this phenomenon as *Displaced Mother's Syndrome.* The displacement often occurs when she becomes aware that in having followed The Scripted Life, the needs and wants of her Authentic Self have been displaced by those of her consumer self. Summing up the issue from wide range of economically, socially and religiously diverse women who have shared their thoughts with me on this topic... *I grew up doing what I was supposed to do. Getting the right grades, going to the right school, joining the right organizations, getting the professional degree, finding the right husband, moving to the right zip code, aligning with the right peer groups, and having the correct number of children and pets. I have methodically checked off each item on my how to live a happy life checklist. Although I love my family, and it looks like I have a great life, I am unfulfilled as a person. How did I get here and what is it all for?*

Note that the recurring word above is *right.* The question is, *right* for whom - your Authentic Self or consumer self?

It has been fascinating to observe how many women have followed the scripted path that gave rise to what I call D.M.S. Step one, be involved an contribute. Often expressed by joining as many local boards and committees as possible - school, philanthropic, religious, etc. Step two involves permission to give to oneself. This can take any form, including exercise, therapy, meditation and personal projects. If one is still unfulfilled, step three entails returning to the comfort of our conditioning by going back to school for yet another degree to find refuge in work.

Conflict can arise at any point during this process as a result of attempting to serve and explore her own needs, as well as the needs of her family, which often run at cross purpose. If you are a *good* mom and follow the Scripted Life, you will do what you are *supposed* to do and displace or sacrifice your own needs and wants for family, spouse, children, possessions, peers, your god, your religion, and so on. The resulting dynamic is one where your existence is defined externally, not internally.

One explanation for this phenomenon is that many of us were conditioned through society's consumer based value system, rather than being educated in creating our own, personally developed value system and **Guiding Principles**. One based on honestly understanding who you are, and how to best express YOU. Sit with this concept for a moment. Do you know what that would look or feel like? Can you distinguish where your societal conditioning ends, and your Authentic Self and its needs begin?

Don't Look For External Solutions to Internal Problems

Our purchasing decisions often reflect consumer conditioning, rather than the Authentic Self. As such, our consumer value system has conditioned many of us to make it a priority to accept whatever fashion style reflects the *Social Currency* of the moment. Regardless of how it fits or objectively looks, many feel it is more important to be perceived, counted and included as a relevant member of the consumer herd, finding safety and validation in its numbers.

Some people feel a powerful compulsion to be acknowledged for wearing the *right style* or *label*, even if it does not fit well, look good or honestly express themselves. This is because The Scripted Life of a consumer requires our validation and approval be acquired and reinforced through external sources.

While speaking on the pressure of young women to present a flawless, idealized image of themselves via social media, Jane Buckingham, founder of the Millennial-focused research firm Trendera says, *"So many women treat life as a constant status update. They're thinking about how their lives look instead of how their lives feel."* You nailed it Jane!!

Some of you may be thinking, if my goal is happiness, and feeding my consumer self makes me happy, so what? Mission accomplished! If you have gone through a process like **The Reflex**, and discovered your Authentic Self is truly living The Scripted Life of a consumer, then go for it.

At least in part however, most of us seek refuge in our consumer selves to fill the personal void of our unmet needs and wants. Our addictive consumption comes in many forms including alcohol, other drugs, sex, food, work, TV, video games, social media, mobile technology, and all forms of shopping and purchases.

Do you feed your consumer self to distract you from the other areas of your life you are not happy with? To some degree and for most people, the answer is yes, which is one of the reasons many of us struggle long term, with goals and happiness. When our goals and happiness are tied to external forces not aligned with our Authentic Self and Guiding Principles, the Thoughts, Words and Actions we produce will not support inner peace, fulfillment and happiness.

As a result of this misalignment, your happiness is likely to be short lived. The consumer self has a limited capacity to support meaningful, long term happiness without the internal support from Guiding Principles and the Authentic Self. Each time you attempt to acquire personal fulfillment through your consumer self, further conditions and reinforces your dependence on these external sources to get your happiness fix. As with any addiction, you will soon adapt to its effects making it more difficult to feel satisfied, requiring greater levels of future consumption.

High Waisted Jeans

While discussing back to school clothing with my wife and daughter this year, my wife brought up high-waisted jeans, to which my daughter replied, *I don't like them.* I followed by commenting that high-waisted jeans are not flattering on most people. My wife responded by laughing and saying to my daughter, *so daddy thinks he knows fashion now.* She followed this by saying, *high-waisted jeans are back in and very fashionable.* She then rattled off a list of notable fashion icons who were wearing them, along with quotes from a few fashion gods proclaiming they are now *in.*

First of all, it is not THAT funny I was commenting on fashion. One area of my expertise lies in evaluating and developing bodies, of which proportion, symmetry and bio-mechanics are key components. How clothes fit on each body are powerfully governed by these factors. Second, our differing perspectives highlight the central issue as to what motivates our purchasing decisions. Are they derived from our personal observations, expression and self discovery, or are we powerfully influenced to reflexively react the way the industry has conditioned us to shop and feel about clothes?

In making my case against high-waisted jeans, I stated I understood the sales pitch, what they are *supposed* to do. *Create a visual elongation of the legs, while accentuating the distinction between hips and waist.* That's the fantasy. The problem is that in reality, they often don't. Not even on many models, who typically wear it better than most.

High-waisted jeans have to fit perfectly to flatter and achieve their stated objectives. If they are too loose, too tight or too long (gap or sag), they simply don't look right. It is at one or more of these points the fit fails for most people.

On the fence, but not completely convinced, I challenged my wife to look at people wearing these jeans with a pair of fresh eyes, applying the criteria above. This meant she needed to consciously disconnected from the sales pitch and what she has been conditioned to believe about them. After taking my challenge, she reevaluated her position, and as of this date, we do not have high-waisted jeans in our home.

An amazing transformation took place during this seemingly insignificant conversation about high-waisted jeans. My wife had an engrained, conditioned belief, constructed by advertising, about the value of an article of clothing , how it fits and therefore, its perceived value. The fact *everybody is wearing it* reinforced its validity and claims. Incredibly, when she re-evaluated some of the same people she formerly held up as examples to support her case for high-waisted jeans, she determined they were not flattering, as she had originally believed. Said another way, my wife looked at people, some of them the same people, from two different perspectives and perceived them in two different ways, to form two different conclusions.

In effect, we often see what the manufacturers and advertisers want us to see, even if it runs counter to our personal observations and thoughts. I disagreed with my wife's accepted belief, explained the three points at which they fail for most people (too loose, tight and/or long), and simply asked her to look at people again, but this time NOT through the eyes of a conditioned consumer.

This is the powerfully persuasive art of association. High-waisted jeans advertised on a model or actor who has the correct proportions to flatter the jeans, creates the reflexive association in your brain between sales copy and the image in front of your eyes. Association creates faulty cause and effect relationships as high-waisted jeans cannot cause you to look different than you are. If you have the right physical proportions the jeans require to fit correctly, then this alignment will produce a flattering look. Without this alignment, it is a miss.

Errors in Cause and Effect

We make the error of association and faulty causation in the world of health, fitness and nutrition more often than not. Many people still believe swimming, running, dance, pilates, yoga, power lifting or crossfit will transform them into that visual body type. Dance, barre and pilates style classes are famous for using persuasive language such as *develop long, lean, toned muscles.* Unless it is in your genetic and physiological template, this simply is not true.

Most elite swimmers have a similar look because they have the genetically arranged bio-mechanical proportion, physiology and neurology required to move most efficiently in water. Those who are shorter limbed, have a proportional trunk to lower body length, greater bone density, with thicker, shorter and more plentiful muscle fibers are not built for competitive swimming, and do something more conducive to their predispositions, such as competitive crossfit or power lifting. As with one's character, the activity or situation does not create or define the person, it merely provides an opportunity to uncover what already exists underneath and allow it to be expressed.

As well, take a look at an aerial shot of any large marathon and you will see many people who don't look like they exercise at all, yet have been running for years, often having run many marathons. Yet, due to their predispositions, will never come close to transforming their bodies into the gazelle like forms of the elite runners in front of them.

If the lens through which we look at ourselves and the world around us is manufactured by consumer driven values, then we will see ourselves and the world in a completely different way than when viewed through a lens crafted by the Authentic Self. If what we choose to see and are conditioned to see, are not aligned with the **Guiding Principles** of our Authentic Self, then it becomes incredibly difficult to create Thoughts, Words and Actions to support our happiness and goals.

So, the next time you are tempted to quickly jump on the next trend, piece of technology or fashion style of the moment in the name of feeling good, achieving your goals and finding happiness, it is important to **Check Your Mind**, and determine whether you are looking through the eyes of your Authentic Self or your consumer self.

Since cause and effect are always in play, our purchasing decisions provide an opportunity to express and reinforce the Authentic Self, or the consumer self. Thoughts, Words and Actions reflected by your Authentic Self enable deposits to your subconscious that support happiness and fulfillment. While expressing the consumer self may provide you with short term, *Self-Grasping* benefits, they ultimately prove to be hollow if they are not aligned with your **Guiding Principles**.

It is hard to show honest compassion, without understanding the true nature of your habits, behaviors, priorities, and why you do what you do in life. Take the time to go through the steps of **The Reflex**, to honestly discover the truth about who you are, your Authentic Self, distinct from society's reflected version of your veneer. Through this process, you will uncover your personal path to creating a fulfilled and happy life.

"Happiness is when what you think, what you say, and what you do are in harmony." Mahatma Gandhi

Chapter 7

Compose Yourself

There are many different ways to **Compose Yourself**. Over time, I encourage you to mold and shape this exercise, and create variations to best integrate into your daily flow. When you do, please share your insights with our online community at ChrisWeiler.com.

The basic format I explained in chapter one, is to use 2-3 blank sheets of paper, and begin writing as fast as you can whatever is in your head. DO NOT judge, worry about grammar, punctuation, legibility or try to force your writing to be about anything specific. This is a free flow, subconscious mind dump, from your head to paper. Curse, be profane, prolific, happy, angry, sad or silly. Let whatever is in you flow uninterrupted from pen to paper. Feel free to begin by writing how weird you think this exercise is. What you write does not need to make sense, and might look or *Feel Like* inane ramblings - it's all good! When finished, shred or file your writing and move on with your day.

Ideally, you should always shoot for 3 pages, as it often takes this amount of space to go deep enough to loosen the entrenched thoughts and deeply embedded baggage deposited in your subconscious mind. At times however, you may be genuinely done after 2 pages, and have nothing else to write. There are also times when you are short on time and simply need to stop. That's okay, as the process of changing behaviors and habits is an endurance event, NOT a sprint.

Feel proud and satisfied you took the few moments you had to **Compose Yourself**, rather than justify blowing it off because something else came up, and you plan to *do it later*. Of course there are times when this will happen, so **Check Your Mind** to honestly distinguish between your legitimate and illegitimate reasoning.

Checking Your Mind is a powerful tool for *Checks* and *Balances,* as you work through changing your reflexive behaviors. Apply it liberally!

Not Just for Adults

This is an all ages exercise. My daughter began **Composing Herself** in 6th grade. She will begin 9th grade this fall and does this on her own whenever she feels stressed or needs to clear her head. She says she feels an immediate difference which is why she keeps doing it. I didn't realize she continued doing this on her own until I walked in on her about 6 months ago **Composing Herself**. As this is a private exercise not to be interrupted, she simply says *I'm writing,* which means *don't interrupt my flow, we'll talk when I'm finished.* Rock On! I am SO PROUD!

I don't do a lot of wishing. I do a lot of doing though - Katy.

This quote is from a model in the Summer 2014 issue of the women's apparel magazine, Title Nine. This magazine incorporates a cool feature called Title Nine Quotes, which gives personal information about the models such as interests, vocation, avocation and lifestyle perspectives. Interestingly, the *models* Title Nine uses, are not models by occupation. Rather, Title Nine sources their talent through friends, and friends of friends, who actually engage in the athletic activities they are photographed doing. Their *models* occupations range from small business owners, to school teachers, veterinarians to civil engineers, and attorneys to homemakers. I'm sharing this background information about Title Nine because they exemplify a business whose philosophy and practices are in complete alignment with their **Guiding Principles**.

Katy's quote above resonates with me, as I developed **The Reflex** to enable us to move beyond self-discovery, wishes and goals, and TAKE ACTION in achieving whatever is personally meaningful in our lives. *That's interesting* and *I never thought about that,* are two responses often used to signal little will get done or change. Restricted to information that only lives in the mind, rather than mixing with the heart.

Action Steps

Another, powerful way to **Compose Yourself**, which goes beyond a *subconscious house cleaning*, is to integrate action steps into the process. Action steps are bridges that connect thoughts, goals and plans to their manifestation in reality.

Sure, you have plans to quit smoking, stop procrastinating, get married, get divorced, start your business or lose weight. So, what actionable steps have you taken to bridge the gap between your schemes, dreams, and desired outcome?

FIRST

Check Your Mind to discover what you think or feel when you are stressed, angry, depressed, aren't being productive, procrastinating, or experiencing any Thoughts, Words or Actions that oppose your goals. There is no right or wrong answer, simply an honest unveiling of the subconscious triggers that create obstacles between you and your happiness.

SECOND

Name the thoughts and/or feelings and write them down on a piece of paper. Be Concise, choosing as few words as possible.

THIRD

Choose one or more words that counter or oppose the thoughts and feelings you wrote above and write them down.

FOURTH

Building Bridges. Write down ONE action step that physically connects you to your goal and moves you one step closer to integrating it into your life. Ex. Sign up for class. Get up and run a 1/4 mile. Make that call. Commit an **Act of Compassion**. Now write this action step over and over until you fill up the page. When finished, get up and do it - NOW!

Repeat the process tomorrow with another action step.

Why This Works

This version of **Compose Yourself** adds the additional element of **Action Steps**. Since many of us get bogged down at this critical juncture between thought and action, this exercise enables us to successfully bridge the gap.

Breaking Down the Four Action Steps

1. When you **Checked Your Mind**, you discovered what you thought and felt.

2. You liberated your discovery from the dark recesses of your mind and exposed them to the light of day, concisely writing down what you thought and felt. There is a marked difference between the thought, word, image or feeling held in your mind, and those same things seen reflected back at you when viewed with your eyes. This makes it tangible and therefore, more difficult to ignore or dismiss.

For example, the image we hold in our mind of ourselves or another person, is often a bit different than the reality we see reflected back in a mirror, or viewing the other person face to face. Law enforcement reserves a bit of skepticism for eyewitness reports, as they understand the longer an image or details of an experience is held in the mind, the more likely it is to be recolored and reshaped, by having its details subtly altered each time it is referenced.

This phenomenon is also seen in the Telephone Game, where one person tells a story or describes an image to the person next to them, who must then repeat it as accurately as possible to the next person. Although everyone tries to retell the story with precision, it is inevitable that most people alter some detail(s) that changes the story from its original form.

When someone tells us a story or shares information, we reflexively color it with our own personal frame of reference. A frame of reference is best understood as a lens each of us views the world through. Each of our lenses is primarily constructed from Our life's experiences and conditioning that leave deposits in the subconscious mind are what give rise to each of our individual frames of reference. As a result, our frames of reference give rise to our perspectives, outlook and point of view.

3. In the third step, we apply a bit of cognitive replacement, by exchanging the thoughts and feelings that oppose our efforts, with thoughts and feelings that support our efforts. This is a powerful technique, that works especially well when other techniques such as visualization fall short. As an aside, this is a powerful technique to use with athletes.

4. This final step connects your thoughts and feelings that support your efforts, with ACTION. Yes, it is that important that the word needs to be shouted, as the only way we get things done is by taking action. I cannot impress on you enough how vital ACTION STEPS are to your success.

The Problem With Self-Help Advice

Although it is common to feel inspired, motivated and energized while reading self-help books or attending seminars, those feelings are often short-lived as most people merely borrowed the speaker's or author's words of empowerment without learning how to generate them from within. Consider the concept of *Give a fish, feed for a day. Teach to fish, feed for life.* As a result, when your experience is over, those feelings quickly dissipate as you reflexively defer to your core conditioned behaviors.

This phenomenon is commonly seen in students who understand the material presented during a lecture or while being directly tutored, but are unable to apply it later. Although the student has understood the basic concepts as applied to the specific problems presented while in the presence of the expert, they have not internalized the root, foundational principles required to extrapolate and apply it to different problems presented in the future, such as a test.

Worse still, those feelings of empowerment can actually disable you from taking action because at the root level, all you wanted was to feel good, or find a port in the storm to shelter you from the challenging areas in your life. Self-help experiences often provide this type of temporary refuge.

My point is twofold. First, unless you have an actionable plan and TAKE DAILY ACTIONABLE STEPS towards your goals, you will likely continue the common pattern of moving from one self-help experience to the next, always struggling with your same issues. Second, understand that we can only be motivated from within, not from other people or experiences, unless what you feel is anchored to an internally driven value such as a **Guiding Principle.**

That's the secret sauce!

Chapter 8

I Don't Wanna...

I DON'T WANT TO DO THINGS

This and the following chapter will cover the prevailing two reasons why most of us struggle with habits and behaviors that oppose our goals, success and happiness. The first one I call *I Don't Wanna* or *I Don't Feel Like It.*

Our basic rational for why we do or do not do something, has not changed much from when we were 5 years old. When we are young and don't want to do something, we simply say, *I Don't Wanna!* When pressed further for an answer, we have one additional layer of introspection available by explaining, because *I Don't Feel Like It.*

Regardless of our age, the reality is that mostly we do something because we *Feel Like It,* or don't do something because we *Don't Feel Like It.*

As adults, we think with the prefrontal cortex, the brain's rational part. In our youth, we process information with the amygdala, the emotional part. This explains why as kids, we don't need a rational explanation beyond *I Don't Feel Like It.*

As an aside, it is this gap between the emotional and rational centers of the brain that explains why there is much drama with kids, especially teens. The emotional centers of their brains turn the volume up on their daily experiences. An adult says, *hey I just saw Sam,* while many tweens and teens say, *OMG, I JUST SAW SAM!!!!*

Although the emotional and rational centers of the brain typically balance themselves out by age 25, our reflexes are still largely tied to a feeling, or at first, a gut reaction, which is followed and then often tempered by our rational brain.

You are only a page and half into this chapter and I'm sure that in some form, many of you have already considered, *I'm an adult, with responsibilities and obligations not only to myself, but to my family, friends and co-workers. As such, I do many things that "I Don't Wanna" do on a daily basis.* At first glance, it might appear that my logic is flawed, so let's dig a little deeper into this process.

Take a moment and think of your daily responsibilities and obligations, the things you do for others. Part of this list will undoubtedly include things you *Don't Feel Like* doing, but do anyway. I challenge you to explain why you do these things, without using the words *I, ME, MY, OUR,* or including any benefit to yourself, whether physical, mental or emotional. You will find this a nearly impossible task.

If you find an exception, please share it at ChrisWeiler.com

This exercise essentially references the age old philosophical debate of whether one can truly commit an act of pure altruism. Pure altruism requires a completely selfless act.

I don't believe a truly selfless (removal of self) condition can exist, as there is no way to untangle yourself from your intent and action. Said another way, you cannot remove your physical, mental and/or emotional self from your actions.

So, the concept of altruism is as inherently flawed as questioning whether you can eat yourself. Yes, I said eat yourself. Again, we find ourselves met with an impossible condition, as eating oneself requires the mouth and digestive system to both eat and be eaten. Although a silly example, this thought process provides us with an opportunity to dig down to the roots that support our behaviors and habits.

What about when you give your time, money or well wishes to complete strangers, isn't that a selfless act? If you **Check Your Mind** before, during or after those acts, you will discover that you generally feel good, satisfied or fulfilled. If you burrow down a bit further, you will discover this is because your Thoughts, Words and/or Actions are tied to a **Guiding Principle** that you care about or *Feel Like* upholding.

Perhaps this **Guiding Principle** to give, was conditioned or inspired through your family, friends, community, religion, personal experiences and/or personal enlightenment. Regardless of how or why, the fact remains that your giving to others is important to you, something you care about, and what prompts you to act, which is why it cannot be a selfless act. You act, and in doing so fulfill a personal need, regardless of how others benefit.

Caveat Emptor?

What about when your actions cause other people to lose? Those who harm others, also do so because they *Feel Like It*. The difference is that these people, whether criminals or not, have a different set of **Guiding Principles**, created and reinforced by a different set of values.

A client of mine who used to work for a large investment firm, told me how she observed a subordinate of hers on the phone, deriding an elderly client for investing her retirement savings with him, which he mostly lost.

After the call ended, my client confronted him about his behavior and ethics. His response, *F@#K her! If she's stupid enough to let me talk her into investing all her money with me, then she deserves to lose it and I deserve to have it!* Like I said, my client used to work at investment firms, but after many grotesque expressions of these types of *principles* and *values*, she finally chose another industry as these practices did not align with her Guiding Principles and Authentic Self.

Parents Often *Don't Feel Like It*

As parents, we are often in the position of doing things we *Don't Feel Like* doing. I *Don't Feel Like* driving my daughter to her friends house, spending six hours at a gymnastics meet, track meet, choir concert, violin recital, going to school fundraisers or chaperoning her school field trips. Okay, the field trips are usually fun.

I do however, *Feel Like* supporting one of my **Guiding Principles,** to guide in the development of a compassionate, happy, healthy, thinking person, that I love with all my heart. So when she asks me to drive her to a friends house, I put my *attention* on the *intention* of contributing to my daughters happiness and healthy social development. When I align my Thoughts, Words and Actions with my **Guiding Principle**, I actually feel happy about spending my time doing something I otherwise would not *Feel Like* doing.

However, if my daughter asks me to drive her somewhere and my reflex is to sigh, get up and proceed to do so, with a heavy, resigned air of merely fulfilling one of my parental duties, then I make a low value deposit to my subconscious mind, which does not align with my **Guiding Principle.**

You Work for Money!?

Although this might be hard to believe, it has been rumored there are people who work for reasons other than pure joy, personal satisfaction or an obligation to contribute to our society. Apparently, these renegades work primarily to earn money. The ability to provide food, clothing, shelter, security, and acquire life enhancing goods and services seem to be the primary drivers.

Humor aside, whether or not you *Feel Like* going to work, you do so because you *Feel Like* receiving the benefits it provides for you and the people you care about, who you *feel* responsible and obligated to.

To be clear, we do what we *Feel Like* doing, within the context of our physical, mental and emotional resources. Obviously a prisoner, whether a criminal, or of war, does not have the freedom to do whatever he *Feels Like*. But in context of his specific circumstances, he does do what he *Feels Like* - good or bad.

Similarly, those in abusive relationships often stay because they don't *Feel Like* they have a choice. In the end, their actions and inactions are the result of what they *Feel Like* doing. It is also an example of what happens when our **Guiding Principles**, goals and the Thoughts, Words and Actions that support them, are not in alignment. Of course the person being abused wants to be happy and doesn't want to be abused, yet their Thoughts, Words and Actions do not support this goal, because they do not *Feel* as if they have options.* Although the circumstances and consequences are vastly different, we can apply this exact same thought process to weight loss. Align your feelings with your **Guiding Principles**, to support succeeding at your goals.

Now that I've established we are creatures who basically do what we *Feel Like* doing, Let's circle back and explore how *I Don't Feel Like It* shapes our habits and behaviors, which ultimately undermines our goals and happiness. This is the result of an incongruity between what the mind wants and the heart feels it needs.

---

*Please do not interpret my comments on abuse as being insensitive or implying it is "their fault." This is not my intent. I am merely referencing the established and well documented model of abuse. However, if you found yourself thinking this way, it is another opportunity to practice **Checking Your Mind** and ask, was that on his mind's side or mine? Every action/reaction is an opportunity for us to learn about ourselves.

Social Currency

As a culture, we have been conditioned to want things many of us don't innately want. Advertising, marketing and media have a profound impact on how we think, feel and act. Our hair, face, teeth, body, clothing, accessories, mobile technology, occupation, car, home, zip code, children, schools, pets, the words we choose, where we shop and what we buy, are all subject to external judgments, policies, advice and social conditioning. It is not surprising that these items represent where we spend the majority of our time, focus, energy and money. Collectively, these areas of our lives represent our *Social Currency*. Even more restrictive than money, *Social Currency* not only has a value limit, but also a limitation on where it is valued and who will accept yours.

Social Currency is powerfully bonded to one's feelings of being relevant. and therefore a powerful determinant of what we *Feel Like* and *Don't Feel Like* doing. It requires constant attention and support as you are mostly judged on your most recent deposit. Wearing the wrong label, not speaking in the approved vernacular, driving the wrong vehicle or associating with the wrong people will quickly bleed your Social Currency account dry in the eyes of those who value that currency. Due to its insatiable appetite, Social Currency requires a powerful anchor, often quietly depositing itself as a **Guiding Principle** in the subconscious mind, where it creates self-sustaining Thoughts, Words and Actions. As Social Currency represents the external you, what you do for others to see, it is rarely capable of aligning with your Authentic Self.

The Paris Hilton Effect

I coined this term in 2005 to describe the nature of *Social Currency*. How it is interwoven into the fabric of our society, our economy, and how this in turn can create a disconnect between our goals, resolutions and the actions we take to achieve them.

Back in the day, when a club wanted to attract hip 20 something's to their grand opening, many would hire Paris Hilton to show at their opening. Like moths to Paris' flame, she attracted those who believe they have the same *Social Currency* as Paris Hilton is portrayed to have. Those who think they have the look, style, and swagger, would make sure they were seen at that club's grand opening. Whether or not they actually wield the same *Social Currency* is not relevant, as it is all about the show, the impression, or *Theater of the Mind*. They merely need to be perceived, or at least, feel as if they are perceived as having the required currency.

The Paris Hilton Effect is one of perception. It enables you to be instantly identified by other people who value the same *Social Currency*. It is an unspoken language that is used to label, tag and categorize like with like. Replace Paris Hilton with whoever fills this ubiquitous role as the poster child for *Social Currency* at any point in the future. Perhaps the Kardashian Effect is more fitting in 2014. Five years from now, insert the name that will be their replacement. Recognize that *Social Currency* has a powerful subconscious influence over what we *feel* and *don't feel like* doing.

We Crave Attention

When we peel the layers off The Paris Hilton Effect, we reveal the core objective - to receive attention. The need to be acknowledged, relevant, seen, counted, and included, is a powerful driver that can impact nearly every decision in our consumer driven lives. This results in our being conditioned to look for motivation, and behavioral change tools outside of ourselves, rather than develop them from within.

Unlike the rest of the animal kingdom, one of the universal struggles unique to our species, is that we are often conflicted between what we want and what we need. Our ego and consumer driven lifestyles have conditioned us to yearn for wants that mostly do not reflect what we need to be happy at the individual level. This creates habits that make us primarily focus on the benefits - what we get. We crave attention because of the benefits. In turn, any product or service that promises to increase those benefits, gets our attention.

Many of us struggle with our place in this world because we attempt to solve our internal issues with external, consumer driven solutions. One explanation for this is that our consumer conditioning has not educated us in *how* to internally acquire benefits, only products and services, which by proxy are supposed to provide us with the benefits. The market sells us on the idea of what we need and the benefits we will receive. In response, we demand more products and services to provide those benefits and the market complies.

Till Death Do Us Part

The divorce rate statistics in the United States are at best a crude estimate, as compiling accurate data and drawing valid conclusions in this space is particularly difficult. In addition, its numbers are often manipulated by those with political, religious and/or marketing agendas. The media likes to spin an exaggerated 50 percent divorce rate, while the most accurate data available puts the number around 20 percent, with divorce of second marriages between 60-70 percent. Ask most adults in this country what the divorce rate is and many will parrot *50 percent* or *1 in 2 marriages end up in divorce.* *Consumer conditioning* and *common knowledge* strike again.

This number is simply based on half as many divorce filings versus marriage filings per year. It is flawed statistical analysis to simply measure yearly marriages against divorces, and hope to find an accurate divorce rate percent. Regardless of whether it is 1 in 2 or 1 in 5 marriages that fail, there are a lot of people who are unhappy enough with one of the biggest decisions in their lives to dissolve the relationship. Furthermore, whatever the actual divorce rate is, cannot reflect how many additional people are unhappy in their marriages, yet choose not to divorce.

My point is this. If you choose to make possessions, assets, what you acquire and with whom you are affiliated with, the principles that guide you on your path to happiness and the good life, then make sure you are being honest about what you, as an individual, require to feel happy and fulfilled. It is vital that your life's script is written by you, and not a fairy tale storied in your mind while growing up, with edits provided by consumer marketing, political and religious agendas, of an ideal that does not match YOU.

In my capacity as a trainer for the past twenty years, the most predictable event I have witnessed is divorce. Like clockwork, as soon as the last child has graduated high school, the divorce papers are filed. Even after the acquisition of the right house, spouse, kids, pets, occupation, clothes, cars, boats, events and vacations, they realize after many wasted years there is still a void, which leaves them fundamentally malnourished. The consumer driven lifestyle is often misleading as it can be fun, exciting, egolicious (yep, a made up word), and at times serve as a port in the storm to shelter and distract from the needs of the Authentic Self.

Your Mind's Side or Mine?

Every situation, action and reaction, is an opportunity to discover something about the nature of ourselves. Therefore, I encourage you to **Check Your Mind** to discover what you reflexively think and feel about what I have written regarding consumerism, and *Social Currency*.

Do you agree, disagree, feel defensive, offensive, enlightened, intrigued, indifferent, or think I am being overly harsh, judgmental, or otherwise negative? Now determine if the results of **Checking Your Mind** are on your mind's side or mine. Am I expressing myself the way you think I am, with the intent you think I have, or is your perspective colored by your personal frames of references, which do not accurately reflect my values or intent?

This important dynamic is often at the root of miscommunication. The point of this exercise is to consider the following two questions, especially when there is a conflict, during any verbal or non-verbal communication with others: *Do your conclusions reveal more about yourself, than they do about the other person or situation?* Was the misunderstanding due to *what you said* or *how you heard it*? **Check Your Mind.**

Did you actually say something offensive to me, or did I mistakenly think or feel you offended me? If I have a reflexive habit where I silently or verbally criticize people and circumstances throughout the day, I am much more likely to pass what I hear, read, and see through a filter of criticism. Depending on the nature of what I am hearing or reading, I am much more likely to read criticism in, because my frame of reference colors my experiences with criticism. The significance of this concept is clear when we remember the conscious mind draws on our subconscious frames of reference for our reflexive Thoughts, Words and Actions.

The Reflex is a deconstruction/reconstruction process. Can you think of an example where any deconstruction or reconstruction process is not to some extant messy and inconvenient to yourself or others around the process? It is simply in its nature. The value of the mess, noise, pain, joy, and inconvenience, is that we feel something. It is in the feeling space we find our Authentic Self and our path to happiness.

Yet Another Weight Loss Comparison

Let's turn our attention again to weight loss, to understand the power *Social Currency* has in establishing our habits and behaviors. Unless you have a metabolic, physical, or hormonal disorder, or have limitations from certain prescription medication, you lose weight because you want to lose weight.

Conversely, if you cannot lose weight and maintain it, you simply *Don't Feel Like it* - enough. The motion goes with the emotion, and we are motivated to do what we *Feel Like* doing.

That's right, I said if you cannot lose weight, and keep a personally acceptable amount off long term, then you honestly do not want to achieve your weight loss goals bad enough. More specifically, you are not emotionally invested enough to *feel* sufficiently motivated to alter or create a lifestyle that supports your goal. Sure, you want the end result, the benefits, but not bad enough to put in the required effort. You might think it would be great if you owned your own business, but are you willing to do what is necessary?

Most people are not, which is why there will always be another fat loss Tip, Trick or Hack available for your consumption.

Many of us want one or more of the following conditions: To be rich, skinny, strong, healthy, fit, fabulous and happy. As I said earlier, the problem is that many of us simply want the *Social Currency* the end result provides. Yet, *how* we apply ourselves in any endeavor, is where our power for change lives, and is directly related to the quality of our results.

So, I want to lose weight, get strong, fit and healthy. Thankfully, there is a never ending supply of magic bullet products and services that are continually marketed and advertised through both traditional and social media channels. A consumer conditioning process, reinforces a fantasy that I should not have to exert much effort to achieve these goals. Quite a thoughtful process to first try and condition my value system so I feel I need or want these things, and then manufacture products that are designed to be perceived as filling those exact wants.

Finally, I can shut my brain off and coast through life. What's that Mr. Huxley? What do you mean... a Brave New World?

I do not promote the victim mentality described above. I also do not believe that free individuals can be conditioned without their consent - it is a partnership and a choice.

Consider the words of Socrates, *The unexamined life is not worth living*. If you don't stop, think, and consider the impact of the Thoughts, Words and Actions that contribute to your reflexive behaviors and habits, then expect to be conditioned.

My favorite supplement infomercial of all time was called "Exercise in a Bottle." *Don't waste your time exercising, when you can get the same exercise benefits while you sleep, with Exercise in a Bottle.* That's right, a magic pill you take to get fit while you sleep! Brilliantly crafted language designed to excite our cultural magic bullet mentality. Since mobile technology is now a permanent fixture in our lives, we now have opportunities to be conditioned everywhere we go. I'm visualizing a mobile-marketing intravenous drip.

As I said at the beginning of this chapter, not much has fundamentally changed since we were five years old. If we are being honest and precise, many of us don't even place much value on the end result, which is why we struggle. Instead, we value the *Social Currency* tied to the result. We covet the benefits. Again, it is all about *the show*. The nod of approval, the attention, the look, the feel, what we can wear and how we wear it. This dynamic applies to every area of life. At the moment, we happen to be discussing weight loss.

Passion perseveres. It is what inspires both beautiful creation and horrible destruction. Passion is what enables us to do, and there can be no passion without inspiration, and no inspiration without feeling.

The same rules apply to business. The business owners and serial entrepreneurs I know, share a common love for the feelings they experience when creating business processes, testing sales techniques, brokering deals, and making money.

Land of The Free, Home of The Consumer

Whether you know it or not, we have all been subject to a Pavlovian style, consumer conditioning process since around 1950. Sure, the infrastructure was built out during the 1920's, but the depression, followed by the next world war, disrupted that progress for a while. Our post World War II government made it clear that our primary function as Americans were to be *consumers*. It was at this point, we were again sold the American Dream and became a nation of consumers. We were conditioned to want the home with the white picket fence, kids, pets, cars and *the finer things in life.*

Get an education to land your 9-5 job, where you leave for work the same time your neighbors do, are home for supper by 6pm, mow your lawn on Saturday and attend religious services on Sunday. Although installment credit had been available since the 20's, the post WWII era saw the rollout of revolving consumer credit, and forever changed how we consume.

We were also sold on technology liberating us with the 4x4 plan. Technology would enable us to have a 4 hour work day, 4 day work week. Sold again in the 70's, 80's and 90's, to convince us to jump on the current technology bandwagon. I think we can all agree we have fallen a bit short of that goal. Like jumping the Grand Canyon with a bicycle short.

On the other hand, I can text, play games on my phone, and be on call for work 24/7, so... there's that.

Mass print advertising was leveraged to show housewives bright, shiny appliances and clothing they should want for their new home, while promoting automobiles, lawn mowers, tools and other gadgets that should be important to men.

Radio, still used today and effective to a point, has obvious visual limitations. Radio advertising influences listeners through a technique they call *Theater of the Mind*, which requires a greater level of attention paid by the listener to be persuaded and conditioned. So, the most powerful move was to leverage the evolving audio/visual medium - Television. We can thank our government for modern television, as they gave up the necessary frequency bandwidth, as part of an initiative to deploy it as a vehicle for consumer spending.

Behavioral psychologists have known for a long time that people spend money to consume products and services when they feel good and happy, and don't make as many purchases when they don't feel good. This explains why many car dealerships still display huge inflatable monkeys and dinosaurs on their lots. Some might drive by and think it's silly, but silly is still a good feeling and makes you smile inside. It is hard to imagine someone getting irritated or depressed when seeing a smiling, 50 foot inflatable monkey.

Since it was understood that people open their wallets when they feel good, the plan involved the broadcast of feel good TV shows, while advertising targeted goods and services through commercials. So began a new era, in training a generation in consumer lifestyle and spending, values and habits. These behavioral consumer habits have continued to be passed along and reinforced with each successive generation to present day. Although the format of television and the types of shows aired have changed, the basic model and purpose has not - consumerism. Work, spend, repeat.

Don't misunderstand, my objective is not to condemn capitalism, free enterprise or our culture. Remember, this book is called **The Reflex**. Anything that is tied to our reflexive conditioning, is especially important in learning how our behaviors and habits support or oppose our efforts in achieving what is personally meaningful. Consequently, it is essential we understand the core that many of our reflexive behaviors are tied to, enabling us to better address and manage them.

Having this context helps us effectively sort through questions such as, *Are those products, body styles, ways of being, choices and actions really important and meaningful to me, or am I just trained to be dissatisfied with who I am and what I have now?*

Slowly chew and digest the last part of the concept above.

**Am I just trained to be dissatisfied with
who I am and what I have now?**

The majority of people who do not succeed at losing weight or getting their dream body, typically suffer from their goal not being internally driven, but externally driven.

Many people simply want *body beautiful*, or at least an acceptable, trendy, marketable *look*, because our society places a high value on that currency. It is one of the reasons why networks and advertisers love reality TV shows. As you watch, you are conditioned to place a high perceived value on everything you see. The homes, cars, clothes, bodies, jewelry, events and parties, along with what and where to eat, drink and shop. The other reason, reality TV shows are one of the cheapest formats to produce.

What Drives Your Value System?

Are your goals internally driven by your personal value system, or externally triggered by our culture's *Social Currency* or consumer driven value system? Internally driven processes typically succeed because they are anchored to and supported by your heart and how you feel - your Authentic Self. This is the path that enables you to access your power for change. Externally driven goals are typically not sustainable because they are only important, relevant and meaningful, when in the presence of the external triggers they are tied to, whether people, places or objects. When detached from these triggers, what do you personally care or not care about? What do you, with no external considerations, *feel* or *don't feel like* doing?

While watching television, looking at advertising, shopping, or observing someone who is carrying the same *Social Currency* we have been conditioned to covet, we are reminded by whoever is doing the selling, of what *should* be important to us.

Yet, exercising and eating properly long term can rarely be maintained through external processes. Sure, you can buy and wear some piece of technology with high *Social Currency*, which wakes you up, counts your steps, calories, tracks your workouts, and probably predicts the eye color of your first born child. The truth however, is that none of these *externals* can put your heart and passion (feelings) into the process. Guess what? Those feelings are why the person exercising next to you, or on the same diet, going through the same physical motions, gets the results you don't. This is true for any goal, like quitting smoking or pulling yourself out of depression. How you feel and internalize your goals, affects how you think, act and for weight loss, your metabolism.

Many of you who struggle with weight loss, nutrition and exercise, don't want the end result for you, but do it because you are supposed to want it. In reality, you do not want to or like to exercise, or eat well with any kind of regularity. Although you dutifully go through the motions, you are not fully invested in the process or lifestyle. Be honest, if society did not place such high Social Currency on how you look, many of you would feel quite comfortable and not think twice about being 5-25 pounds overweight.

I will say it again, when our internal self and processes are aligned with our goals and principles, we succeed. In achieving what is important, the value system we subscribe to is not as important as the feelings that support our Thoughts, Words and Actions being in alignment with our principles. This is what creates the motivation to *Wanna Do It*.

This is a powerful mark of distinction, as internally driven goals are always with you, tied to and supported by your feelings, which fuels your determination, motivation and passion. Internally driven goals enable you to *Feel Like* creating tiny bridges that connect one progressive step forward to the next. It is this series of connected bridges, each one alone insignificant, which successfully connects you from goal inception, to goal completion, personal satisfaction and happiness.

Without purposeful intention to drive your goals, you are detached from what you feel, your heart. If you do not *Feel Like* taking action, it is because there is no **Guiding Principle** to plug your purposeful intent into. As a result, you must rely on your existing habits and conditioned reflexes, which are not set up to empower your success. These conditions typically lead to failed goals and resolutions.

Emotion Creates *Motion*!

Chapter 9

Tips, Tricks and Hacks

This chapter exposes the second most significant reason why most of us struggle with habits and behaviors that oppose our goals, success and happiness. Consider the examples given in this chapter, as to why we are so enchanted with *Tips, Tricks* and *Hacks*. The next time you **Check Your Mind,** ask yourself if any apply in opposing your efforts or distorting your perspective.

Nearly every day I receive requests to provide *Tips, Tricks* and *Hacks (shortcuts)* for fitness, weight loss, nutrition, fear, stress, motivation, mindfulness, procrastination and productivity. Last month I received one asking for tips on how to be happy in 10 minutes or less. Really!? As if happiness were a light switch to be turned on and off at will, or by pressing a few buttons. Rather, it is the indirect by-product of specific Thoughts, Words and Actions expressed over time, which contributes to the development of general happiness and achieving our goals.

I recently received a request for *tips* and *tricks* on how to have *The Talk* with your kids. If you have not had the foresight, and taken the effort to develop general bridges of communication with your children from day one, it will not be there for you to cross when you want to drive The Talk vehicle across. For those of you who say, *my kids won't talk to me*, re-read the previous sentence.

What happens when our addiction to shortcuts, couples with the wants, desires and goals of our conditioned consumer mindset? Well, they produce offspring that are reflexively susceptible to *Tips, Tricks* and *Hacks*.

Learn this one trick to lose belly fat.

Tips on how to score. (Maybe I'm talking sports, maybe not).

5 tips to improve motivation.

5 tips to decrease procrastination.

Tips, Tricks and *Hacks* exist to beat stress, be happy, find love, make up, break up, stop smoking, eat less, eat more, lose weight, get ripped, reduce wrinkles... and the list goes on.

I know, YOU are never seduced by these pitches - I'm talking about *other people*. While reading the examples above, you are removed from the event and can therefore look at them objectively, with a rational mind, and convince yourself *I'd never fall for that!* Yet, from within the situation, in the heat of the moment, the rational centers of the brain soften.

For simple task based processes, you may find that employing short term tactics, like only checking email or returning phone calls at specific times, help provide a more efficient flow to your day. We cannot however, take a shortcut through the complexities of development, changes to behaviors and habits, or management of people and processes.

Although shortcuts alone do not have the capacity to create something valuable, or significantly contribute to your long term success, they are not without value as they can augment a solid strategy.

Tactics vs. Strategy

We can easily understand the problematic nature of *Tips, Tricks* and *Hacks* by looking at tactics versus strategy. Tactics, much like *Tips, Tricks* and *Hacks*, are tools best used to make adjustments or enhancements while deploying a strategy or development process. Once a strategy is developed, it can be enhanced by certain tactics, but one can rarely succeed long term, or build something meaningful by using tactics alone. Unconvinced? I invite you to a game of chess. You can rely on tactics, while I employ strategy.

Tips, Tricks and *Hacks* have an exceptionally alluring appeal in our technology driven, magic-bullet culture. They are typically short, simple, disposable scraps of information we can text, tweet, or post, without having to exert much effort, or go too deep within ourselves.

The sender and receiver benefit, as they feel a sense of accomplishment, and greater connection to our social media construct. Yet, if we are being honest, there is a part within many of us that love the idea of getting what we think are secrets or insider information, as it makes us feel *special*. Keep in mind my thoughts in the previous chapter on craving attention, and on page 23, regarding *Self-Grasping*.

Of course, some *Tips, Tricks* and *Hacks* can be useful, such as keyboard shortcuts, how to unclog a drain, or remove a stain. The difference is that *Tips, Tricks* and *Hacks* are not in themselves, substantial enough to support anything that requires development. Yet, they are often sold and consumed specifically to avoid going through a developmental process, or anything that requires much effort. Guess what? The most important areas of our lives require development and effort, including education, fitness, health, relationships and career. As such, you cannot *Tip, Trick* and *Hack* your way through them. Those who try, find their return is commensurate with their investment.

How did those *tips* on pick-up lines and dating work for you? Is your investment portfolio managed through *Tips, Tricks* and *Hacks*, or do you employ a strategic approach?

Id's All About The Ego

A few years ago, *Jail-Breaking* your phone or other piece of mobile technology got you mad *Social Currency*, especially from the Apple community. Many people engaged in this activity envisioned themselves as warrior hackers on the battlefield of technology. The reality is that this *Jail-Break* unlocks a few low level optional functions such as extra apps, memory or wallpaper. Not exactly the stuff of legend. Sure, some might think, *Dude, lighten up, we're just trying to inject a little fun into our day.* Fair enough, but let's take a moment to follow this *fun* you speak of down the rabbit hole.

We were out to dinner with friends the day the latest iteration of the iPad was released. My friend, whom I will refer to as The Warrior, regaled us with his tale of how he made sure he ordered his and his daughters *pads* so they arrived on the actual Release Day. However, when The Warrior's wife decided she also wanted one, it was too late to place another order to arrive in time. Obviously, everyone not having their own new iPad on Release Day is unthinkable - we're not savages. Let's face it, not having it on Release Day, when everyone else involved is having a communal, uni-mind orgasm, celebrating the slightly updated, gift of technology bestowed to us, greatly reduces its perceived value. It just occurred to me... is *Release Day* is a euphemism?

Perhaps I will **Check My Mind** on that later. For now, let us get back to The Warrior's tale.

So, in what can only be described as an act of chivalrous bravery, with no consideration for his own safety, The Warrior took off work, to track and hunt down his prey and bring the fabled iPad back for his fair bride. And, after briefly waiting in line for a little over 4 hours, The Warrior did just that.

Well... after he went to another store and waited in yet one more line, to also buy one for his mother in law, as the first store would only allow a single unit purchase.

All puffed up after such a thrilling day of battle, you understand why The Warrior needed food, drink and merriment, in the company of both friends and strangers, who would marvel at his heroic deeds.

In doing this, The Warrior felt he made a significant deposit to his *Social Currency* bank account. *We've come a long way baby!*

Again, if we are being honest, what motivates us to go through this kind of *fun,* is the ego, the Id, and the need to feel as if we are part of something socially relevant. Ironically, if there were not so many hoops to jump through or long lines to stand in, we would not value the purchase or process as much. It is in this ironic space, that reveals the true nature of our motivations and the value of our acquisitions.

Don't misunderstand, my objective is not to judge right or wrong, but to help provide you with an introspective platform to challenge and expose the authentic nature of your

Thoughts, Words and Actions that support your intentions and motivations. They must first be exposed to determine if they support or oppose your objectives and align with your **Guiding Principles**.

On page 81, I describe how we figuratively go into battle each day with a latent warrior mentality. Role playing and first person perspective video games, especially first person shooter games, have only further promoted this distorted vision of ourselves as technology warriors or heroes. There is in fact, a well known website for internet marketing called Warriors Forum. It has been common practice for the past 15 years for marketers, programmers, software and technology developers, to borrow heavily from military parlance to describe the way they envision themselves in their activities. *Brute Force* and *Trojan Horse* are among the many commonly used terms in the information security industry.

I realize some of you will not be able to relate to my remarks above regarding technology warriors and video games. Not a problem, as you don't need to be part of that world to understand its relevancy. YouTube is the second most searched for and viewed website in the world. What do you think is the most popular YouTube personality or channel? Videos of major recording artists, fitness, the Khan Academy or those cats in shark costumes that ride on Roombas? No. As of 2014, the most watched person, with the most subscribers and popular channel, is a guy that comments on the game play of video games as he plays them.

The New Hero?

In her iconic book Atlas Shrugged, Ayn Rand describes *man as a heroic being.* I think the conscious and subconscious minds find it quite challenging and disingenuous to assign the term *heroic,* to a society consumed by screen resolution, sound bites, the latest app, reality TV, specialty coffee drinks, and the development of 10 year old girls who are already conditioned to ask, *Who are you wearing?*

Unfortunately, Ayn Rand's vision of a hero is often reduced to a person with a mobile device in one hand and flavored drink in another, attempting to draw attention by projecting the illusion of doing something important, or *on the go.*

The Pain/Pleasure Paradox

Our deluded self-images, and projections of our personas, distorted through a hand held screen, often serve to distance ourselves from understanding what is necessary to live a personally meaningful, fulfilled, happy life.

Unfortunately, this dynamic mostly serves to deepen our consumer conditioning, as it reinforces a skewed pain/pleasure relationship. The more we allow ourselves to be conditioned to *Tips, Tricks* and *Hacks,* the greater pleasure we extract from them, and more dependent we become. This happens as a result of it reflexively decreasing our tolerance for more in-depth processes, which creates a *pain* (intolerance), or at the very least, the absence of pleasure.

So the meaningful, introspective, developmental part of our existence becomes the path of *Greater Resistance,* while *Tips, Tricks* and *Hacks* become paths of *Least Resistance.*

The danger, is that your Thoughts, Words and Actions are deposited to your subconscious mind, and therefore, what is available for the conscious mind to withdraw. This shapes your habits and behaviors, which gives rise to your future Thoughts, Words and Actions.

If these support your personal principles and goals, rather than society's consumer oriented goals, you are on your way to a meaningful, fulfilling, and happy life. However, if they oppose your personal principles and goals, or mostly satisfy society's consumer driven, or *Self-Grasping* goals, you are on your way to something else.

I think it is worth considering, one reason we place so much importance on these *Self-Grasping* events, is that it is a coping mechanism of the heart and mind, in an attempt to help justify the time we spend on such low value actions. We need to believe we are engaged in relevant and sometimes grand events, when our intent and motivation often serve to merely fill time, take refuge from our day in meaningless distractions, or bolster one's *Social Currency.*

It is as if this heroic being Ayn Rand speaks of, is now relegated to serving low-level daily functions, which do not have the capacity to nourish the heart or spirit.

The effect is disheartening to watch, as the hero attempts to squeeze some sense of satisfaction, meaning and enjoyment, from his high resolution, hand held device. A device that is a perfect vehicle to reinforce a consumer mindset, while further conditioning him to embrace a purpose that is largely about the acquisition of *Social Currency*.

His Thoughts, Words and Actions do not shape or govern the device. Rather, it requires him to bend, twist and mold his Thoughts, Words and Actions, to conform to its inflexible design and nature. Nor can the hero impose his will on the device in any meaningful way. Instead, he is forced to make concessions at every other turn, as the technology trains him in how he needs to express himself through a device ultimately designed as a sales funnel for future consumption. From this perspective, it is easy to understand why many people feel unhappy, unfulfilled and lost. This also may partially explains our ravenous appetite for the next version of our beloved devices. *Maybe the next version will fill the void.*

Addicted To The Crutch

If it makes you feel good, even briefly, why is it low value? Similar to the use/abuse cycle of any addiction, it feels good in the moment, but is short lived, and soon you will need another dose. Addictions serve as crutches, as they support that which is too weak to internally support itself. Used too long, a crutch becomes the *Path of Least Resistance*, while you increase your dependency/addiction.

In context of this discussion, the only way to get back that same feeling is to again drink from the consumer well, or try the next *Tip, Trick or Hack.*

Tips, Tricks and Hacks are Cheap and Disposable

Another problem is that *Tips, Tricks* and *Hacks* have an extremely limited shelf life. They lose their effect because of how well we adapt. Initially, *Tips, Tricks* and *Hacks,* bypass or side step our conditioned reflex. This effect creates a neurological disruption, similar to whacking your knee on a table, which distracts you from your already sore elbow. As soon as your body processes the signals being communicated from your knee, you are once again reminded of your preexisting elbow pain. Similarly, you can try to *trick* your body into limiting the amount of food you feel you need to eat, by drinking water before your meal. Unfortunately, your body will soon adapt to this *Trick* you received in the form a *Tip,* to *Hack* your fat loss, and will lose effectiveness.

I recently read an article on *tips* to deal with stress, which suggested turning off the lights when you get home to decrease stimulation. Short term, this may disrupt your stress reflex, but you will adapt, and this *trick* will quickly become ineffective, as your stress reflex is your *reflexive path of least resistance* and therefore, dominant. Remember, the path used most often, becomes the Path of Least Resistance.

What is required, is to establish a *new path of least resistance* to deal with your stress triggers. This action transforms the pathways tied to your stress reflex, from the *paths of least resistance* to the *paths of greater resistance*, and therefore harder to access. The result is a new, dominant reflexive response to your stress triggers. Combine **Checking Your Mind** and the **Compose Yourself** with Action Steps from pages 14 and 97, to establish a new reflexive response cycle.

Not to fear, when dimming the lights becomes less effective at reducing your stress, you can simply go to the Google gods and ask for new *Tip, Trick* or *Hack*. Thankfully we are all armed with mobile devices, so we can acquire *Tips, Tricks* and *Hacks* no matter where we are. Whew! I was almost faced with having to do some meaningful, internal work. Not to worry, technology saved me - again. Excuse me for a moment, I should post this tip online.

Subtle Tools of Self-Sabotage

We subconsciously understand that *Tips, Tricks* and *Hacks* are a low value commodity, as they are sold and consumed as cheap and disposable. Furthermore, there is a disproportionate relationship between the time spent seeking and trying *Tips, Tricks* and *Hacks,* and the degree of progress, development and lasting change one actually makes towards their goals.

A subtle way to self-sabotage our progress with *Tips, Tricks* and *Hacks* is by using them as a distraction, to convince ourselves and others we are doing something relevant, when in reality, we are not. Purchasing the latest weight loss gimmick that you will never use beyond the first 3 weeks, will end the same way it always does. Once the honeymoon period is over, it will be added to your pile of similarly discarded past purchases, as you turn your focus to the next gimmick of the moment.

The problem is that we are conditioned to go for the magic bullet first. Are you only interested in quick and dirty *Tips, Tricks* and *Hacks* that promise fantasy benefits, or would you like to begin a process of development to achieve your goals? **Check Your Mind**, what was your reflex to my question? To be clear, *Tips, Tricks* and *Hacks* can enhance an already thoughtfully developed process. However, they cannot be relied upon to replace or develop a process in the first place.

Interview Tips

Prior to a recent interview, I was given a few tips that included not eating anything flour based, which crunches or makes crumbs, as the remnants can linger in your mouth and throat, creating unexpected dry spots that could promote having to cough or clear your throat. Having a warm beverage such as tea was also suggested, along with limiting the use of weak transitional terms such as *ummm*.

Since I had done the work upfront, by having developed my concept, practiced articulating its process, and answering likely questions, I was prepared to have a meaningful, engaging conversation with the host. *Tips* that help me avoid coughing or getting dry mouth, can only enhance my expression and experience.

Meanwhile, let's imagine an alternate universe, where the host informed me afterwards that I gave a poor interview and I replied, *But I followed your tips?! I didn't eat anything crunchy, had warm tea by my side and tried not to say Ummm much!* The host responds, *those tips were not meant to replace you having done the work to properly prepare yourself on your topic. You did not sound very confident, and it was very hard to follow you, as you were struggling to find words to articulate yourself. On top of that, you were not really engaging or having a conversation with me, but merely rambled on as if you were giving a speech - A poorly written one.* Remember, *Tips, Tricks* and *Hacks* are not the preferred tools when constructing meaningful areas of our lives.

The Veneer of Efficiency is Inefficient

One way we have adapted to our current state of information overload, has been to create burdensome shortcuts in our communication. I say burdensome, because the net effect of our *shortcuts* typically results in taking more time to manage the process or technology.

Added to this, is the greater time spent rectifying the miscommunication from these time saving processes and technologies. Rarely have I hired a programmer, graphic artist, or marketing person that does not suffer from poor communication skills. This is often due to the fact that a common shortcut today is to not read an entire email, but only the first few sentences to *get the idea* of what is being communicated.

It would be a mistake to dismiss or underestimate the effect that media sound bites, texting and social media posts confined to 140 characters or less has on conditioning our shorter attention spans.

Aren't we being more efficient though? No, as this mostly results in decreasing our tolerance to sustained focus and attention to detail (pain/pleasure paradox).

Understand, I set expectations from the start that communication is extremely important to me. I state that every word I write to them has a purpose and is relevant, or I would not have taken the time to write them (keep in mind my *Efficiency Principle* from chapter 1).

Yet, with the exception of my current website developer and book cover designer, Gion-Per Marxer, I have always been disappointed. I can't tell you how many times I have had to say, *did you read the entire email? Read it now, while we're on the phone.*

The standard response, *Oh, I guess I didn't read that far.* My standard reply, *I hired you to carry out specific instructions, not get the idea or gist of something.* So, their *shortcut* results in an inefficient, multistep process, resulting in many emails, frustration and finally one or more phone conversations, to accomplish what should have been a one step process.

The *thing* Has No Power - You Do!

For many people, *Tips, Tricks* and *Hacks*, along with the never ending supply of mobile gadgets, keeps us engaged in activities we actually don't *Feel Like* doing. In our push button society, we love to give our powers for personal care and development to *things* that exist outside of our bodies, hearts and minds - mobile technology and apps. When we are internally driven or motivated, we don't often need to look outside of ourselves for this type of support, because when we *Feel Like* doing it - we do it! Motivation results from what we *Feel*. When we require some type of external support or crutch every step of the way, we merely prop up an internal system unable to support itself. As the crutch strains against the internal resistance of how we honestly feel, *I Don't Wanna* or *Don't Feel Like* doing it, we never truly embrace the goal or lifestyle with the heart. Similar to long term use of a crutch for a weak leg, it mostly breeds dependence and disability.

There is only one difference between those of you who have wanted to start a business and those who took it from concept to reality. Those who took action, *Felt Like It* more than you. Motivation comes when you *Feel Like* taking action.

Most of these external crutches, the *Tips, Tricks* and *Hacks,* are a poor choice in tools, as they temporarily distract you from the truth - you *Don't Feel Like It.* Since you have not addressed the root issue and aligned how you feel with your goals, the struggle is always there, looking for an opportunity to pull you back and derail your efforts.

This misalignment wastes energy, focus and rarely has the power to create lasting behavioral change. You can choose the right tool to drive a screw into the wall, a screwdriver, or struggle with a hammer that will oppose your efforts by creating a lot more work and mess. The end result of which cannot be counted on for long term support.

Of course, there are some of you who have launched a personal fitness campaign, centered around a piece of wearable mobile technology. Giving you *tips,* feedback and motivation throughout the day has contributed to you achieving your health and fitness goals. Well done!

Not to be rude or pessimistic, but let's chat in five to ten years and see where you are then. Was it a short term, disposable goal, anchored to and therefore only sustainable through an external device, or a long term lifestyle change?

Check Your Mind. How did you digest my question? Why? What does your answer tell you about yourself?

The *thing* Has No Power - You Do! Your power for change, success and happiness exists within your heart, mind and body, guided by your intention and principles. This is what shapes your Thoughts, Words and Actions. Those who align their Thoughts, Words and actions with their goals and **Guiding Principles**, are able to successfully leverage external support, in the form of *Tips, Tricks* and *Hacks*.

Our Technology Addiction

More than anything else, we live and work to be consumers, and believe we need technology to both help us work and save us from work. When looked at from this perspective, you might say *Tips, Tricks* and *Hacks* are a natural by-product of this dynamic. Aside from work, we mostly use technology to both entertain and distract ourselves from a life not fully expressed. Am I being too harsh? Consider the number one and two answers I receive when I ask people why they spend their time playing games, watching videos and using social media on their phones. #1 *something to do.* #2 a way *to spend time* or *kill time.* The first sentence on the WikiHow.com page titled *How to Play Candy Crush Saga* reads, *Candy Crush Saga is everywhere. For some, it is just a way to kill time.*

In total we probably spend more time than we save, evaluating, learning, purchasing, servicing, and otherwise managing our technology. Especially since it seems we are in a perpetual cycle of public beta-testing the latest tech gadget or software.

This simply means many technology companies release their products for public consumption knowing they are problematic and often without detailed enough instructions, which puts the obligation on the consumer to invest their time figuring it out, reporting problems and communicating with tech support. All this for the privilege of staying current with the latest hardware or software.

Of course we can list some of the positive effects technology is having in certain areas of medicine, production, shopping, and the environment. What about in areas such as education? Increasingly, school districts are allocating funds to supply students with tablets such as the iPad, which mainly serves to make us *look* and *feel* as if we are advancing and keeping up with society's technology driven side of *Social Currency. But an iPad in a low income home helps them be and feel connected.* As if a consumer product has the power to give one confidence or value education in the home. The other obvious problem, many of these families are unable or unwilling to pay for internet service. Consumer driven solutions rarely hit the mark.

The media and product pitches would certainly lead you to believe that these technologies in the classroom and home will keep us competitive and close the achievement gap. Yet, that conclusion is quickly checked by the reality of our international test scores, which continue to GO DOWN. In many instances, the only thing classroom iPads and Smart Boards have accomplished, is to dull the edge on the blade of education in the classroom - the teacher.

But those high resolution screens sure look pretty, and make us feel as if we are advancing and relevant. As consumers, we love shiny new things, a powerful component of our consumer conditioning.

The ability to empower our lives does not primarily exist in the technology or tool, but in the Mind, Body and Heart of the person using the tool. When we align our Authentic Self and **Guiding Principles**, we produce Thoughts, Words and Actions that express the nature and intent of how we apply our tools. These are the primary aspects that separate brilliant, dynamic, inspiring educators from the rest.

The *thing* Has No Power - You Do!
Don't misunderstand, I am not ignoring or discounting the many good deeds, or beautiful personal expressions and contributions made through technology. It is important however, to consider the more we plug into our technology, with a hunger for *Tips, Tricks* and *Hacks*, the more difficult it may become to plug into the Mind, Body and Heart. We cannot shortcut development and introspection.

SOMA

I am going to take some liberties and get a little dramatically prophetic here, so give me a bit of latitude. I am honestly concerned our appetite for *Tips, Tricks* and *Hacks*, our *Magic Bullet* mentality, the burgeoning supplement and pharmaceutical markets, coupled with our insatiable appetite for mood and energy enhancing beverages, is the perfect breeding ground to give birth to a Happiness Drug, similar to the one in Aldous Huxley's Brave New World (1932). Described as *euphoric, narcotic and pleasantly hallucinant,* Soma is the drug a Brave New World uses to control what its citizens *Feel* and *Don't Fe el Like* doing.

The term *happiness* is currently a marketing buzzword. As a culture of consumers, this means we should *think* and *feel* it is relevant and something to be acquired, like a product. This also means *happiness* has high *Social Currency.* If an over the counter supplement came out at 8am tomorrow morning labeled The Happiness Pill, it would be sold out by 10am and many of us would have to wait for backorders to be filled. Ironically, those relegated to backorder status would not be happy.

I think it is interesting to consider there are times when science fiction writers accurately foretell our future reality. I suspect this is due to their ability to extrapolate from our past and especially present, to accurately plot out our future trajectory.

Huxley feared a world in which the truth would be shoved into obscurity by a sea of amusement and entertainment. According to Neil Postman in his book *Amusing Ourselves to Death*, "Huxley feared what we love will ruin us." Judging by today's entertainment-centered world, perhaps Huxley was right. Our culture is not controlled by censorship, but by seeking pleasure through consumption. Interestingly, Soma is the most common brand name of the muscle-relaxant carisoprodol, and was licensed in 1996 by Royce Laboratories, Inc.

My point, habits and behaviors that support happiness, passion, motivation and success are not things you go out and acquire, consume or are given. As well, they are rarely useful wrapped in the form of a *Tip*, *Trick* or *Hack*. Rather, they are the indirect by-products and nurturing of your personal Thoughts, Words and Actions, which create the causes for those conditions. In turn, this leads to a fulfilled and meaningful life.

Chapter 10

Where is Your Place of Refuge?

In Buddhism, a Sangha is one's community. It is a literal or figurative place we go, to seek refuge from the parts of our lives and society that tug and pull at our resolve, increase stress and create obstacles that oppose our values, principles, efforts and focus. Your Sangha is a place to increase the space between one moment and the next... and breathe... contemplate, meditate, and emotionally recharge. Much more than a mere port, to provide shelter from the storms in your life, a Sangha is an empowering **Place of Refuge**, where you can both establish and reinforce your **Guiding Principles.** A **Place of Refuge** is powered by your intentions, which creates Thoughts, Words and Actions that either support or oppose your goals and happiness. You reap what you sow in your **Place of Refuge.**

Connecting with your **Place of Refuge** in person is not always necessary, as merely holding a picture of it in your mind and heart, anchored by your intention, enables you to benefit as well. Consider prisoners of war who keep mentally and emotionally connected to their support community, typically their family. This connection allows them to be strong, empowered and remain focused on their goals, even though their circumstances oppose their efforts.

Whether you recognize it as such or not, we all have at least one **Place of Refuge**. Take a moment now and **Check Your Mind** to discover where your **Place of Refuge** is located. Throughout this book I have told you there is no right or wrong answer when you Check Your Mind, only right or wrong for you. In this instance however, I believe a poor choice for a Place of Refuge, is one that does not align with or support your **Guiding Principles** and goals. If your only Place of Refuge merely serves to distract you from work, or the challenging parts of your life, with no committed Thoughts, Words or Actions that build bridges between you and your goals, then I do not consider it a qualified **Place of Refuge**.

Poor choices for a **Place of Refuge** include:
Your Phone
  Addictions (legal or illegal)
Your Phone
  A Bar/Club
Your Phone
  Television
Your Phone
  Video games
Your Phone
  Internet
Your Phone!!

Do you see a theme here?   Have I been too subtle?

Watching the way people covet, cradle, fondle and otherwise interact with their phones, regardless of what else they are doing, unfortunately makes mobile communication technology the most common **Place of Refuge**.

Up until now, you may not have considered the relationship you have with your phone Pavlovian, but take note of how often you check in with it, and the way you reflexively react to its chirps, dings, tones and vibrations. Interrupting face to face conversations is commonplace when your phone beckons. Those who lose their phone or otherwise choose to take a break from it, often report a loss of security and reflexively check for it throughout the day as if it were a phantom limb. Not since Charlie Brown's blanket toting pal Linus, and the inseparable relationship with his blanket, have I seen such a co-dependent relationship.

I know... *you can stop anytime you want.*

Empty Calories

The problem with using mobile technology as a **Place of Refuge**, lies in the intention that drives how we use our phones. With heads down, blocking out the rest of the world, including traffic while driving or walking across the street, we focus on playing games, watching videos, and listening to music, often while intermittently texting or talking. In and of themselves, there is nothing wrong with the general nature of these types of entertainment.

The danger however, is that many people reflexively use their personal technology to extract a short term, feel good, emotional fix, to compensate for areas of their lives that are malnourished, similar to the multiple caffeine pit stops made to *get us through the day*. The underpinnings of this dynamic are the same as when reaching for external support from a drink, cigarette or other social lubricant or crutch. Instead of reaching within your Mind, Body and Heart to help you more fully understand, express and empower yourself, you reach outside of yourself for some type of support. This process is often debilitating, creating dependency as it weakens the system being *crutched* or supported.

The *thing* Has No Power - You Do!

Generally, crutches are meant to be used as short term bridges, supporting that which cannot support itself, while you work on conditioning and restoring full, self-supporting function. When used too long and guided by the wrong intention, crutches become *The Path of Least Resistance*, reinforcing a cycle of de-conditioning and dependence on their use.

Like spackle used to fill cracks and holes in a wall, a similar dynamic is seen in those who fill the void in their lives with *comfort food*, or mindlessly fill their mouths with *empty calories* from foods such as chips, crackers, candy or cookies. It is not the food item that is the issue, but the intent behind your choice to reach for the *empty calories*. This is what determines the value of the experience and its outcome.

The *empty calories* provided by many technology and food sources, serve as a distraction that interferes with your ability to discover your Authentic Self, and what opposes your efforts at personal fulfillment. The inherent nature of *empty calories* is that their consumption leaves the mind, body and heart malnourished and therefore, still hungry. This hunger creates the causes for a dysfunctional feeding loop, constantly going back to feed on technology, food or other addiction of choice, with the same hollow results.

As a result, we feverishly attempt to *feed the need*, looking for next piece of technology able to do more and give us more options, yet miraculously, also be perceived as a time saving device, which will enable us to *keep up*. The pace of evolving technologies makes us *feel like* we need to continually run faster to play catch up, while in reality, falling farther behind. What I have just described is a classic cycle of dependency and addiction. Common to all addictions, is the extreme difficulty in putting first, the needs of anything that is not the object of your addiction. It is only about you and your needs, as an end in itself. Therefore, for most people, mobile communication devices are a weak **Place of Refuge.**

Are You Feelin' Me?

As we discussed earlier, feelings are what drive our intentions and motivations, creating Thoughts, Words and Actions to express them. The path to achieving goals, making/breaking habits, and creating a meaningful, happy life is about Feelings.

Your **Place of Refuge** should be connected to the rest of your life on an emotional level. Use it to empower you and others in your life, rather than using it in an attempt to block, or dull the pain from the other less desirable parts of your life.

Finding Your Place(s) of Refuge

Remembering *Happiness is in The Details*, let me be clear about the criteria for finding your **Place of Refuge**. Under most circumstances, a **Place of Refuge** should not be chosen as a result of running away from another part of your life. No hiding. Instead, make your decision based on a place you want to run towards and embrace, because it enhances the rest of your life. I know quite a few people who work hard to manage their schedules so they are able to go straight from work to attend meditation and study group once or twice per week at our local Vajrayana Kadampa Buddhist Center. Contrast this **Place of Refuge** with going to a bar, having a few drinks at home, playing games or watching television.

Although there are many creative options in choosing your **Place of Refuge**, it needs to satisfy the requirement of establishing and reinforcing your **Guiding Principles**. The secret is to place your *attention* on the object of your *intention* and **Check Your Mind** to make sure they are in alignment with your **Guiding Principles**. This is how you use your time in your **Place of Refuge** to shape your future Thoughts, Words and Actions to support your goals and happiness.

Important Enough to Repeat

The secret is to place your *attention* on the object of your *intention* and **Check Your Mind** to make sure they are in alignment with your **Guiding Principles**. This is how you power your **Place of Refuge** to meaningfully enhance your life. It is also how you are able to turn most experiences, provided they have the inherent capacity, into a **Place of Refuge**. Inherent capacity means some part of its natural design allows for you to discover and address the qualities within you and your life that oppose your happiness and the happiness of those around you. Alcohol, television and your phone for example, do not have the inherent capacity that allows for you to place your *attention* on the *intention* of aligning your Thoughts, Words and Actions with your **Guiding Principles**, in support of your personal goals and happiness.

What will work however, is using your time while travelling home from work, whether by car, train, bike or while walking, as a **Place of Refuge** before going to your softball game, restaurant, bar or club. This chapter is not about removing the things from your life you currently enjoy. Continue indulging in drinking, gaming, food, social media, the internet and work if this is what helps you feel joy. Do Not however, use them as primary **Places of Refuge**.

Make A Place of Refuge Anywhere

In sharing the following everyday story, I will illustrate how I chose a **Place of Refuge** in the simple act of returning someone's shopping cart to the store for them.

While leaving the grocery store a few weeks ago that does not provide cart corrals in its parking lot, I noticed a woman parked next to me who had her hands full loading her car with groceries and her 3 small children. It took an instant for me to recognize three things. First, she was not in a great position to return her cart. Rarely does anyone lazily leave their cart around the cars in this specific parking lot for someone else to deal with, so I was confident she would be conflicted about leaving her kids in the car to return the cart to the store front, about 40 feet from her vehicle. Second, my returning the cart would be the most efficient action for both of us, as it was temporarily blocking my car while she was loading her kids. Third, I anticipated my action would put a smile on her face, take the edge off and simply make her feel good.

So, without hesitation, I too action. Her response to me asking if I could return her cart for her was the kind of relieved smile we express when someone has taken the weight of an obligation off our shoulders as she said, *thank you so much, that would be wonderful.*

Let's see how this story applies the concepts of **The Reflex**.

1. I discovered my **Authentic Self** through what I believe in and have decided is important to me, having been careful to filter out any unwanted influences of society or religion.

2. My Authentic Self gave birth to one of my **Guiding Principles** - to help others. When in alignment, I am open to seeing opportunities to help others such as the woman with her shopping cart.

3. I **Check My Mind** to verify what I think and feel like doing at that moment is in alignment with my **Guiding Principles**.

4. This alignment creates reflexive Thoughts, Words and Actions to express and take action on my **Guiding Principles,** through **Acts of Compassion,** such as returning the cart.

5. The resulting deposits to my subconscious mind, help create future Thoughts, Words and Actions in support of my **Guiding Principles**. These deposits are now available for withdrawal by my conscious mind to support future Thoughts, Words and Actions that support my goals and happiness. Rock n' Roll!

When broken down to its individual parts, this process might appear mechanical or too involved. In real time however, the time between my observation and decision to return the cart, took less than three seconds.

Technically, a **Place of Refuge** can be nearly anywhere but I think you will find it quite challenging to justify posting updated pictures of The People of Wal-Mart, taking another *Selfie*, updating your *status*, or getting to the next level of Candy Crush, is achieving this objective.

One of my fixed **Places of Refuge** is the gym I built in the former hay loft of my garage. Weights, balls, rollers, ropes, rings, heavy bag, 1,000 square foot rock climbing gym and a big speaker system complete my setup.

During my workouts there are times when I place my *attention* on the *intention* of improving in the areas of compassion, giving, how I communicate with my family, friends and in business. There are other times when I simply play my music loud enough to be heard down the street, and focus on nothing but my workout. It is not as much the activity or the location, but how you apply yourself in whatever you are doing. You can put your *attention* on whatever *intention* is meaningful to you in the moment. Sometimes my *attention* is simply focused on my *intention* of *getting my animal on* during my workout, and nothing else.

Remember - **The *thing* Has No Power - You Do!**

I have also sought refuge in the writing of this book. Breaking down this process in detail and providing personal examples has enabled me to think about and understand both **The Reflex** and myself in a more meaningful way.

Writing this book has been a joy, and I find myself eager to reconnect with it each day, as it enables me to help others and myself.

When I find myself struggling with writing, it is because I have strayed from my **Guiding Principle**. I get back on track when I put my *attention* on the *intention* of helping you achieve your goals. In my heart, I know this benefits us all.

Once you are practiced in the techniques of **The Reflex**, you can use them to reinforce Thoughts, Words and Actions in support of your **Guiding Principles**, habits and goals, while engaged in nearly any activity. For example, Buddhist monks typically start their day cleaning the alter their Buddhist statue and meaningful objects rest on. This cleaning is a ritual they used to convey respect, love, dedication and compassion. Each swipe of the cloth is meaningful as it is used to guide and direct Thoughts, Words and Actions that support their principles. In this way, they are empowering themselves to better generate and share compassion with others.

Your Shower As a Place of Refuge

It was the year 2000 when my daughter was born, and when I began the practice of using my evening shower as a bridge to transition between my life outside and inside my home. Not only was I deepening my commitment to make my family and home my **Place of Refuge**, but also making a specific activity in my home, my evening shower, a **Place of Refuge**. Throughout the day, there are many opportunities to distract and otherwise steer us away from our **Guiding Principles**. As a new father, I had constructed a new set of **Guiding Principles** to reflect the values important to my new family.

My shower ritual simply involved me visualizing, feeling and saying, *as this water runs down my body, it draws out my stress, anger, fears, the pressures of the day, and anything that blocks me from showing my love and compassion to my family. Peace.*

This process is further empowered by placing my *attention* on the *intention* of what is important to me, by connecting my words above, to the physical action of washing and rinsing my body. As I keep my *attention* on my *intention*, I visualize the qualities I want to purge mixed with the water that cascades off my body and down the drain. For me, it is a simple, private, efficient, yet powerfully transformative process.

At times when I know a shower is not practical, I sit in the garage for a few moments and modify my ritual by mixing my words with the sounds and vibrations of my vehicles engine. In addition, I have modified this practice for use while cleaning, strength training, inline skating, ice skating, rock climbing, kayaking, snorkeling, running, and writing this book. In my business I have practiced a form of this since the mid 1990's, immediately before training clients, to help me be *present* and *available* to them.

There is no limit to this practice or what you can create in life. I encourage you to look at yourself and your surroundings as objects looking to collaborate with you, to mold and shape a more empowered, compassionate, happier YOU.

You control whether your **Place of Refuge** is merely a port in the storm you use to hide from the difficult parts of your life, or an empowering place to realign with your **Guiding Principles** and create Thoughts, Words and Actions to feel great in life.

The *thing* Has No Power - You Do!

Chapter 10

Feed Your Body

> **1. Check Your Mind**
>
> **2. Acts of Compassion**
>
> **3. Compose Yourself**
>
> **4. Feed Your Body**

Surprise! There is a fourth step I call **Feed Your Body**, which deals with nutrition and exercise.

Feeding Your Body is not crucial to your success. It should however, be viewed as a step that can augment and provide additional support to your efforts. Simply consume nutrient dense foods, and challenge your mobility and strength. Doing this provides the oxygenated blood supply that transports nutrients to support your body, heart and mind. Indirectly, this helps you remove disempowering subconscious deposits, while boosting your ability to make empowering deposits.

Added to this are the metabolic benefits derived from increased oxygenated blood flow, that helps all body processes function with optimum efficiency.

We are what we eat, is true in the sense that about every three to six months we replace a large percentage of the cells in our body – blood, skin, hair, etc. As such, the nutrients we put in our body literally help shape our future selves.

A strong, mobile, flexible body, can enable you to move through your life with greater efficiency, further develop your cognitive abilities, and increase access to your internal resources. **Feeding Your Body** can bridge the gap between where you are right now, and successful completion of your goals.

Although as a rule you should **Feed Your Body**, there are of course exceptions. If for whatever reason you do not have use of your body due to accident, illness or disease, then obviously you cannot completely **Feed Your Body** in the all the ways I describe. However, I believe this does NOT put you at a disadvantage in changing your habits, behaviors, achieving your goals, and being amazing. Although there are many examples I could use, I'll simply point to Helen Keller and Stephen Hawking - 'Nuff said.

Feeding Your Body deserves a entire book to itself, which is why I chose not to stuff it into these pages. Fortunately, I have written a book that addresses the nutrition aspect of **Feeding Your Body** called **The 3/4 Rule**. You can find it on Amazon or at ChrisWeiler.com. I developed **The 3/4 Rule** to be the easiest and most effective nutrition model available. I show you exactly how to eat for optimal physical and mental performance.

In addition, you will discover how to shop, why all protein is not created equal and how to decode any nutrition label with one simple rule. We'll also dig into those unregulated, expensive, heavily marketed magic bullets - supplements.

The ¾ Rule is not restrictive, applies to all eating environments, and most of what you will find, you have not read or heard before. Although it is target marketed to athletes, **The 3/4 Rule** is for everyone - including you!

Yes, I am pitching another book of mine within this book, **Checking My Mind** however, reveals that my *attention* is on my *intention* to further benefit your life.

Below is a review posted on Amazon.

Okay – I just have to say, "Try it." I am a 50-something female who is not an athlete (although I do get moderate exercise). I read Chris Weiler's The 3/4 Rule a few months ago and loosely applied its approach to my own eating -- not as a test, but more out of curiosity, and not really expecting any particular results.

What I was astonished to find was how much more energy I have to sustain me throughout my day (which I especially appreciated during the busy holiday season)!

The approach is simple, but what I also appreciate is that it is not "a diet." It's an easy, flexible framework for eating, which has prompted me to simply alter some of my choices. It's unlike anything I've heard of or done before. The book is a quick, easy, fun read and gives some fascinating insights into labeling, supplements and more.

Although the book targets young athletes, it is really for everyone. My own experience leads me to think others, perhaps of any age and activity level, may benefit significantly too. Because this little book has improved the quality of my life, I must give it an enthusiastic "thumbs-up" and hope others will read it and be energized

Feed Your Body Online

On my website at ChrisWeiler.com, I have provided helpful tools that further break down and guide you through **The Reflex**, as well as nutrition and exercise for health, fitness and athletic development. I wish for you to feel that my website is a **Place of Refuge**, to keep updated and focused on how to see your goals through to completion, and maintain that empowered feeling that supports a happy, meaningful life.

That's it my friends. I hope you benefit both now and in the future from reading this book, and will begin applying **The Reflex** right now. Remember, simply **Check Your Mind**, perform **Acts of Compassion** and **Compose Yourself** daily to succeed at your goals and create a happy, meaningful, personally fulfilling life.

I'm sure many of you have thoughts or questions, and I would love to hear them. I look forward to connecting with you at ChrisWeiler.com

Before you close this book, **Check Your Mind** to discover what your next reflexive action is going to be. Perhaps eat or go to bed? Get back to work? Put the book out of your mind? Write a glowing review, or begin practicing **The Reflex**?

Regardless, consider whether your next Thought, Word or Action will support your **Guiding Principles,** goals and happiness.

Peace!

About the Author

Chris Weiler is a performance expert to athletes, Fortune 500's and YOU! His background in philosophy, physics, and athletic development, inadvertently helped provide a foundation for his unique perspectives and processes in developing habits and behaviors to maximize personal performance in all areas life. He believes success in personally meaningful actions and goals helps contribute to happiness.

A native of Chicago, Chris enjoys his family, kayaking, rock climbing, 4 wheeling off-road, Buddhism, burning the midnight oil, problem solving and pie. His literary heroic thinkers are Isaac Asimov, Steven Covey, Aldous Huxley, William James, Steven Levitt, George Orwell, Ayn Rand, and Dr. Seuss.